DEINSTITUTIONALIZATION OF DEVELOPMENTALLY DISABLED PERSONS

DEINSTITUTIONALIZATION OF DEVELOPMENTALLY DISABLED PERSONS

A Conceptual Analysis and Guide

by

Valerie J. Bradley

President, Human Services Research Institute
Washington, D.C.

With the assistance of
John W. Ashbaugh and **Mary Ann Allard**

Anne L. Liegey, *Publications Coordinator*
Jerry Evans, *Editorial Assistant*
David Sibbet, *Illustrator*

University Park Press *Baltimore* 

UNIVERSITY PARK PRESS
International Publishers in Science and Medicine
233 East Redwood Street
Baltimore, Maryland 21202

Typeset by American Graphic Arts Corporation

Manufactured in the United States of America by
The Maple Press Company

Library of Congress Cataloging in Publication Data

Bradley, Valerie.
Deinstitutionalization of developmentally disabled persons.

Bibliography: p.
1. Developmentally disabled services—United States.
2. Halfway houses—United States. I. Ashbaugh, John W., joint author. II. Allard, Mary Ann, joint author. III. Title. [DNLM: 1. Child development deviations—Rehabilitation. 2. Community health services—United States. 3. Residential treatment. WS350.6 B811d]

HV3006.A4B7 362.3′0973 78-8281
ISBN 0-8391-1254-8

The original draft of this publication was prepared pursuant to the U.S. Department of Health, Education, and Welfare Contract 100-76-0162.

CONTENTS

Foreword *by John J. Dempsey, Ph.D.* ix
Preface xi

Chapter 1 INTRODUCTION 1
BACKGROUND AND HISTORY 5
IDEOLOGY VS. IMPLEMENTATION 7
EVIDENCE OF INADEQUATE PLANNING 9
Parental Insecurity 9
Hand-Me-Down Financing 9
Angry Caregivers 9
Fluctuating Accountability 10
Love-Hate Relationships with the Private Sector 10
WHAT NEEDS TO BE DONE 11
NOTES 11

Chapter 2 CONTEXT 13
EXPLORATION OF VALUES 15
JUDICIAL IMPERATIVES 19
Involuntary Admission 20
Personal Rights 21
Consent 22
Adequacy of Services 23
Access to Generic Services 24
Implications for Analysis 25
ORGANIZATIONAL STRUCTURE 27
State Developmental Disabilities Authorities 28
State Developmental Disabilities Councils 30
Local Organizations 30
FEDERAL FUNDING 31
Characteristics of Principal Federal Programs 33
Development of Specific State Strategies 34
NOTES 36
APPENDIX: SEVEN MAJOR FEDERAL PROGRAMS THAT PROVIDE FINANCIAL SUPPORT 38

Chapter 3 PLANS 49
CRITICAL CHOICES 51
GOAL DEVELOPMENT 57
NEEDS ASSESSMENT 61
RESOURCE IDENTIFICATION AND DEVELOPMENT 66

ENDORSEMENTS AND NEGOTIATION 72
MONITORING 76
EVALUATION 78
CONCLUSION 81
NOTES 82

Chapter 4 IMPLEMENTATION 83
IMPLEMENTATION MANAGEMENT 88
RESOURCE DEVELOPMENT 91
Use All Available Funds 92
Redeploy Institutional Resources 94
Increase the Level of State Funding 97
Expand the Use of Generic Services 98
Use Less Costly Alternatives 98
QUALITY ASSURANCE 100
Licensing 101
Standard Setting 102
Development of Rates 103
Enforcement 104
COORDINATED CLIENT MANAGEMENT SYSTEM 104
Diagnosis and Evaluation 107
Individual Service Planning 108
Service Procurement 109
Predischarge Planning 110
Monitoring and Follow-Up 112
Advocacy 113
NOTES 114

Chapter 5 SUMMARY 117

APPENDIX I: Bibliography 121
A. General Discussion of Mental Retardation, Developmental Disabilities, Deinstitutionalization, and Institutions and Service Delivery 123
B. Community-Based Issues 125
C. Advocacy 128
D. Costs of and Funding for Residential and Support Systems 129
E. Legal Rights 130
F. Specific State Government Reports 131
G. Bibliographies on Mental Retardation, Deinstitutionalization, and Community Care 136

APPENDIX II: Major Federal Court Rulings 137
A. Prominent Cases 139
B. Selected Cases by Subject 139

APPENDIX III: Values, Ends and Criteria 151

Index 161

FOREWORD

Deinstitutionalization is a painfully long word within which "institution" is the unmistakable root term. The prefix clearly suggests moving away from an institution per se. Beyond that, the term has produced considerable semantic difficulties for all who share an interest in the well-being of the developmentally disabled. The antecedents of deinstitutionalization go back several decades. Improvements in the capability of the community service system represented the first step in the process and the clamor from consumers for access to those services was the second. Third, the introduction of antibiotics reduced the death rate in institutions, and the resulting overcrowding required either building new institutions or finding some community alternatives. Normalization provided the philosophy, and court rulings against unnecessary restrictions in nontherapeutic settings provided the legal ammunition for change. The first usage of the term "deinstitutionalization" appropriately described the efforts to remove people from institutions in favor of something closer to a normal life style in the community.

Many of the early candidates for deinstitutionalization were profoundly disabled and had lived in institutions for most of their lives. The community was too often ill-prepared to care for them in the quantity in which they were discharged. For some, the nightmarish stories of some of the early failures suggested the need to rethink and reconsider. For most others, these experiences pointed to the need for better planning and a broader definition of deinstitutionalization. Indeed the root words implied a "moving away from the institution," but initial experience showed that the meaning had been construed too literally. The focus of planning should be moved away from the institution alone to the entire community service system. Institutional services need to be integrated into a larger and more systemmatic whole. This is the way the term is being used now. It refers to a full continuum of services with the institution at one end as the most restrictive alternative—a veritable revolution in our thinking.

A deliberate federal role in deinstitutionalization, however defined, is still in the making. The driving force at the moment is a report which has come to be called "The GAO Report." On January 7, 1977, the General Accounting Office (GAO) published a report entitled "Returning the Mentally Disabled to the Community: Government Needs To Do More," which focused principally on the mentally retarded and mentally ill. It drew attention to a formidable array of gaps, duplications, inefficiencies, and other consequences of categorical services that have grown incrementally in several federal agencies. The response within the bureaucracy has been quite favorable and the principal agency analyzed, the Department of Health, Education, and Welfare, has created a Task Force on Deinstitutionalization to study ways to implement the recommendations of the GAO Report. Although the full cycle of implementing a rational deinstitutionalization plan at the federal level will likely consume a decade, immediate changes in the nature and volume of the federal role are expected to begin momentarily.

In the meanwhile, sufficient time has passed to begin abstracting from state deinstitutionalization experiences, and this is done in the pages to follow. The unique experience of several states is used to fill out the authors' conceptualization and to test it. The authors' conceptualization of deinstitutionalization is broad enough to be compatible with the expanded definition mentioned above and with the full range of recommendations articulated in the GAO Report. Additionally, it is the most conceptually cohesive approach to deinstitutionalization I have encountered to date, which makes it a much needed benchmark in an exciting, new movement. Although it was originally "pitched" principally to state officials, it should be equally useful for federal and local officials, as well as for classroom use.

Deinstitutionalization will be a dominant social issue over the next decade, and the authors' conceptual approach should be invaluable for the army of professionals who will be involved.

John J. Dempsey, Ph.D.
Public Health Analyst
Office of the Assistant Secretary for Planning and Education
U.S. Department of Health, Education, and Welfare

PREFACE

This book, originally prepared for state officials under a contract from the Department of Health, Education, and Welfare (DHEW 100-76-0162), is written to assist state and local policymakers, administrators, and service providers who have been given responsibility for shifting from an institutional or custodial system of services for developmentally disabled citizens to more dynamic, habilitative, and affirmative modes of care. It is meant to clarify the goals of system improvement in this field and to identify the principal problems of implementation that have bedeviled both program managers and would-be reformers over the past several years.

The creation of community-based services for the developmentally disabled remains primarily a state responsibility, and we believe that this will continue to be true for the forseeable future. Accordingly, we believe that state policymakers, administrators, and service providers must be offered a program of technical assistance based upon the conceptual framework presented in this publication.

The framework enables an understanding of the social, ideological, political, and programmatic factors that have influenced and continue to shape the movement away from large institutions to small community-based settings in the field of developmental disabilities. It provides a mode for assessing deinstitutionalization at the state and local levels by highlighting the context in which these changes must take place, the planning that can assist in directing such change, and the key elements that must be present in the implementation stages in order to ensure a systematic and beneficial result.

It is barely possible, though unlikely, that such a document could have been written ten years ago when only a few states had taken some initial, timorous steps in the direction of deinstitutionalization. Certainly, our work has been greatly aided by reference to the store of experience gained since then. We have attempted to develop our conceptual framework so that policymakers, administrators, and service providers understand and learn from this body of experience. Thus, as part of this framework, we have incorporated state activities exemplifying specific implementation constraints and ways in which states have attempted to overcome those constraints.

The audience for the book is broad. Besides state administrators and legislators, it includes service providers, consumer organizations, and students training to become professionals in the fields of developmental disabilities, social work, psychology, and public administration, or who are studying social policy issues generally.

We would like to take this opportunity to thank all of those persons who volunteered their time to review previous drafts of this report. We also thank our consultants, Tom Joe, Mel Knowlton, Gary Clarke, Nancy Perlman, and Jerry Evans, for their able assistance. And we want especially to thank Jack Dempsey, our project officer, for his guidance and support.

INTRODUCTION
Chapter one

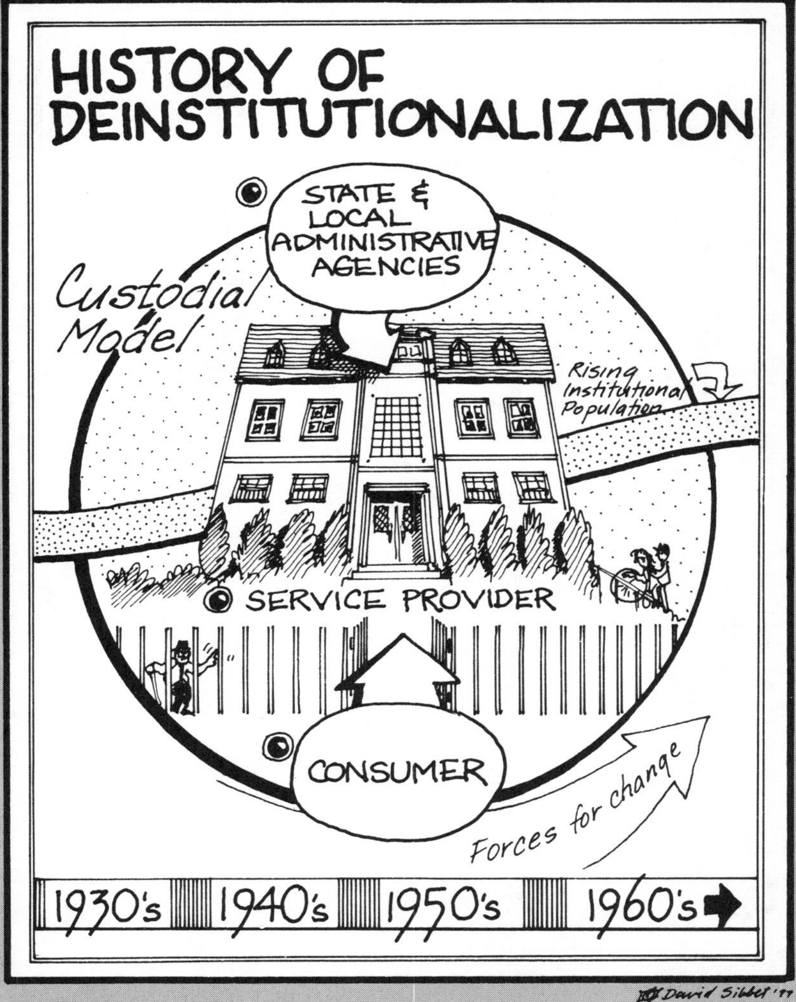

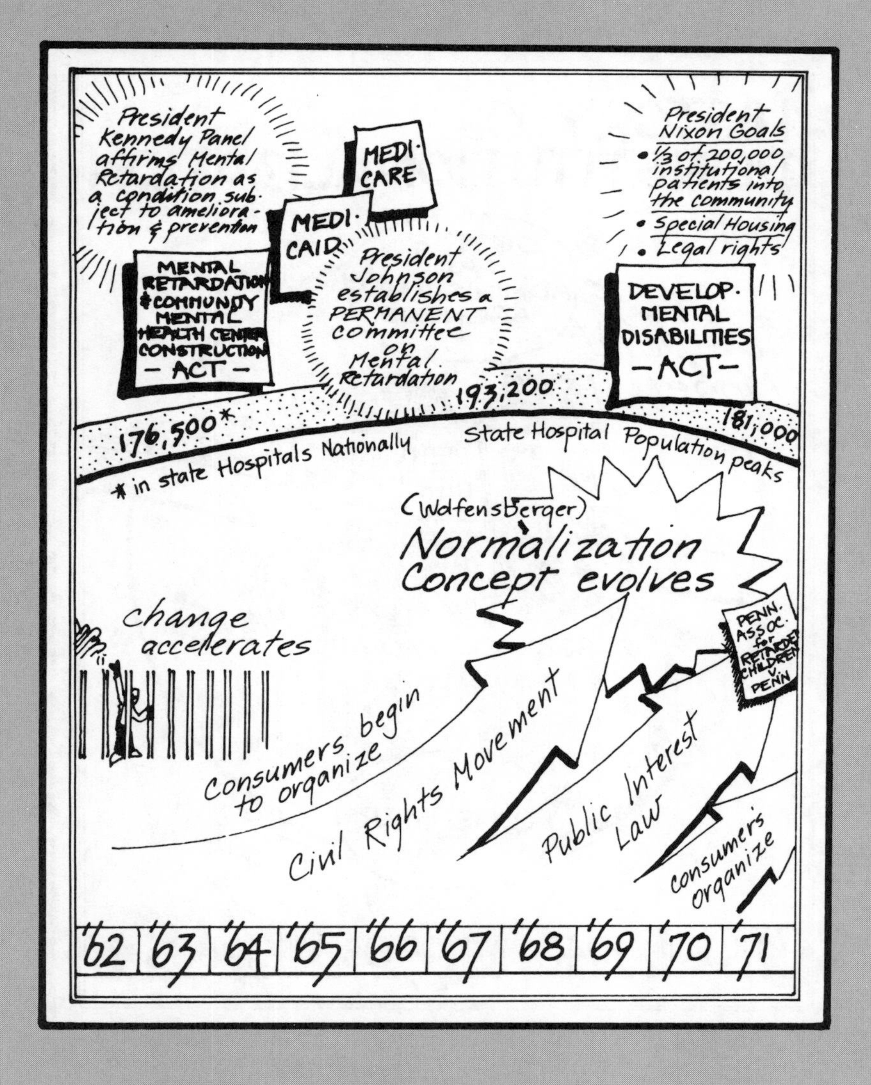

President Kennedy Panel affirms Mental Retardation as a condition subject to amelioration & prevention
MENTAL RETARDATION & COMMUNITY MENTAL HEALTH CENTER CONSTRUCTION —ACT—
MEDI-CAID
MEDI-CARE
President Johnson establishes a PERMANENT committee on Mental Retardation
President Nixon Goals
• 1/3 of 200,000 institutional patients into the community
• Special Housing
• Legal rights
DEVELOP-MENTAL DISABILITIES —ACT—
176,500*
193,200
181,000
* in state Hospitals Nationally
State Hospital Population peaks
(Wolfensberger)
Normalization Concept evolves
change accelerates
PENN. ASSOC. for
v. PENN
Consumers begin to organize
Civil Rights Movement
Public Interest Law
consumers organize
'62 '63 '64 '65 '66 '67 '68 '69 '70 '71

"No discrimination against D.D. in Fed. progs"
President Ford re-affirms Nixon Goals
504 REGS. SIGNED
FEDERAL PROGRAMS
PL 94103 AMENDS D.D. ACT TO SPELL OUT BILL OF RIGHTS & REQUIRE ADVOCACY
DEV. DIS. ACT AMENDED TO INCLUDE LEARNING DISABILITIES
Dynamic Multi-faceted System
SUPPLIMENTAL SECURITY INCOME PROGRAM OPERATIVE (SSI)
REHAB. ACT of 1973 (as amended) FOCUSES ON "Severely disabled"
HEW REGS. for INTERMEDIATE CARE FACILITIES for M.R.
PL 94142 EDUCATION FOR ALL HANDICAPPED CHILDREN -ACT-
STATE AGENCIES
1.8 Million into the community
GROUP HOMES FOR DEVELOPMENTALLY DISABLED
WORK ACTIVITY PROGRAMS
schools
168,300
Population declines
First significant right to treatment case
Better Resource Utilization
Prevent Inappropriate Admissions
Appropriate Community Care
WYATT V. STICKNEY Alab.
Willowbrook case: protection from harm
N.Y. STATE ASSOC. for RETARDED CHILDREN & PARISH V. ROCKEFELLER
WELSH V. LIKINS Minn.
INFANT STIMULATION PROGRAMS
SHELTERED WORKSHOPS
RESPITE CARE FACILITIES
DEVELOPMENTAL DAY PROGRAMS
Suits
Right to treatment
'72 '73 '74 '75 '76 '77 '78 '79 1980's
'77 David Sibbet

BACKGROUND AND HISTORY

There are several milestones that mark the course of reform of the system of care for mentally retarded and other developmentally disabled persons over the past several years.[1] These events have contributed to the small but significant decline in the population of state institutions for the mentally retarded—from 176,000 in 1963 to 168,000 in 1975,[2]—and to the growth in community-based services. The reduction in the institutional population and the change in attitudes and philosophies that it reflects has occurred over a relatively short period of time—short, certainly, in comparison with other social change of comparable significance.

This shift in emphasis away from large custodial facilities has been labeled "deinstitutionalization," a term that only partially characterizes the complex aims of this movement. Today, these aims include the development of adequate and appropriate community residential and support services, the prevention of inappropriate institutional admissions, and the reform of institutional programs.

The impetus for the persistent drive for improved care for developmentally disabled persons comes primarily from an expanded acceptance of "normalization," a principle that asserts that developmentally disabled persons should be served in programs and residences that are as normal as possible.[3] Where this is accomplished, it is presumed that problems of stigma and isolation will be minimized.

In order to understand the complexity of the forces behind this movement, and their impact on the current shape and the content of the system of services for developmentally disabled persons, it is important to take note of the following historical events:

Affirmation by the President's Panel on Mental Retardation in 1962 that mental retardation is a condition that can be prevented in some cases and ameliorated in most others

Passage of the Mental Retardation Facilities and Community Mental Health Centers Construction Act of 1963[4] as proposed by President Kennedy

Establishment of the Medicare and Medicaid programs in the mid-1960s, making it possible for many developmentally disabled persons and their families to secure medical and other long-term care in their communities

Creation of the President's Committee on Mental Retardation, a permanent national advisory body, in 1965[5]

Advent of the civil rights movement, the tenets of which were subsequently applied to many disadvantaged groups, including the developmentally disabled

Growth of "public interest" legal advocacy, which resulted in numerous judicial decisions expanding the rights of the developmentally disabled[6]

Annoucement by President Nixon in 1971 of a national goal to return one-third of all institutionalized mentally retarded persons to supportive community living, together with presidential directives that the Attorney General enforce the rights of the mentally retarded and that the Department of Housing and Urban Development create ways to improve their housing opportunities[7]

Inclusion of a mandate (in the Rehabilitation Act of 1973, as amended) requiring states to address the vocational rehabilitation problems of the severely disabled as a first priority

Creation of other federal programs, including Supplemental Security Income (SSI) and supportive social services (Title XX of the Social Security Act) that provide federal aid for services for the developmentally disabled, among others

In addition, there have been three recent federal actions that will undoubtedly have an impact on programs for developmentally disabled persons. One was the recent promulgation of the regulations pursuant to Section 504 of the Rehabilitation Act of 1973. This provision prohibits discrimination against "otherwise qualified" handicapped persons in any federally supported program. The enforcement of these regulations could substantially benefit developmentally disabled persons seeking jobs, education, and needed services.

A second action, the creation of new standards for Medicaid support for intermediate care facilities for the mentally retarded (ICF/MR), has had an impact that is already being felt. In order to maintain Medicaid support for their institutional systems, many states are being forced to accelerate the movement of clients out of institutions in order to concentrate limited state financial resources on the improvement of physical facilities and staff ratios for those who remain. For example, Georgia and Connecticut are now (1977) in the throes of preparing plans that will eventually reduce their state institutional populations by 500 persons and 750 persons, respectively.

The third recent action was the passage of the Education for All Handicapped Children Act (PL 94-142, 1975), which should have a profound effect over the next decade on institutional admissions and the ability of families to maintain developmentally disabled persons in their own homes.

IDEOLOGY VS. IMPLEMENTATION

The events and actions that have shaped and will shape the system of services for developmentally disabled persons reflect a broad array of philosophical, programmatic, legal, and social visions. They also highlight the foreshortened history of this particular effort at social change. The rapidity with which the values that underpin the system have undergone transformation is in part responsible for some of the discontinuities in the actual application of new principles and theories.

In a sense, the move to integrate developmentally disabled persons into programs and settings as nearly normal as possible is still in its adolescence. Attempts to improve services continue to show little evidence of the strategic precision needed to ensure that changes are successfully integrated into a mature, predictable, and ongoing system. Maturity will come only when actual practice and application catch up with—or at least substantially reflect—commonly held values.

There are many reasons, in addition to the chronological age of the movement, that explain this developmental lag. A major reason, simply stated, is that very few states have taken a systematic view of the implementation of a balanced system of services for developmentally disabled persons.

Lack of a systematic or integrated approach to the improvement of programs for developmentally disabled persons is a major and pervasive constraint to effective action and is traceable to many causes. One explanation derives from factors endemic to the organization of state programs for developmentally disabled clients. The agencies given the responsibility for carrying out the transition to expanded care in the community have been, in most cases, the agencies with primary responsibility for operating the institutional system. Thus, the lead agencies have been forced to reconsider their goals and procedures, and to obtain additional expertise and knowledge in order to understand the complex issues involved in establishing and maintaining community-based resources.

Over and above their lack of experience in the organization of community programs, lead state agencies have been handicapped by their lack of familiarity with and control over other state generic health and welfare agencies. Though the services of these agencies are needed by developmentally disabled persons returned to the community, the agency with responsibility for deinstitutionalization has traditionally had little if any influence over the provision of those services.

This structural problem has been exacerbated by some of the more expedient ends to which deinstitutionalization and its rhetoric have been put over the past several years. In some instances, the client-centered aims of reform, such as maximization of individual potential, have been overlaid with cost-effectiveness arguments suggesting that care in the community is less expensive than care in institutions. Not surprisingly, many state administrators have seized the opportunity to embrace the progressive values of integration and normalization for developmentally disabled persons. They have also promised that client movement from more expensive state institutions to less expensive community programs or facilities, such as nursing homes,[8] subsidized in part by federal funds, would result in a significant savings to the state. Unfortunately, many states found that these two ends were not necessarily complementary, and that clients' welfare suffered when the shift was conducted with an eye to cost considerations. It also became evident that many developmentally disabled persons were merely being moved from institutions operated by the state to smaller ones in the community.

Finally, the maturation of the system of care for developmentally disabled persons has been hampered by a failure to understand the essentially "revolutionary," as opposed to "evolutionary," nature of the changes in care for developmentally disabled persons that deinstitutionalization has come to include over the past ten to fifteen years. Changes in attitude and approach have not come about in an incremental fashion but rather represent, in some instances, a 180-degree turn from the guiding principles of only two decades ago. As a result, some states have attempted to use incremental administrative and management techniques to effect changes that require coordinated implementation across organizational, professional, and jurisdictional lines.

EVIDENCE OF INADEQUATE PLANNING

Failure to recognize the complex nature of the changes being sought has created stresses and strains that are only now becoming evident in many states. These inherent tensions have not as yet brought about a decline in the momentum for reform, but they could prove fatal if not acknowledged and ameliorated. Among the most serious are parental insecurity, "hand-me-down" financing, angry caregivers, fluctuating accountability, and the role of the private sector.

Parental Insecurity

In somes states that moved early to shift resources to the community, and especially in those states that have relied heavily on the private sector for care, families of the developmentally disabled are becoming increasingly anxious about the stability of community services. In California, for example, many parents of institutionalized residents who have been scheduled for return to the community complain that private agencies make no long-term commitment to their children and that such agencies can and do go out of business. Understandably, these parents want some assurance of the state's continuing responsibility for their children.

Hand-Me-Down Financing

Without a systematic approach to the development and expansion of resources, state and local agencies with primary responsibility for developmentally disabled persons have been forced to rely on a variety of financing sources that often impose conflicting requirements and expectations. Lacking sufficient specialized financing of their own or access to generic funding (for housing, job training, etc.), many agencies must continue to rely upon categorical financing that in most cases was developed for groups other than the developmentally disabled.

Angry Caregivers

Rapid moves to reduce institutional programs have too often ignored not only the effect on the clients but also the effect on the institutional employees, many of whom may be forced out of their jobs. Resentful of what may appear to be a denigration of their efforts and fearful of losing their jobs, these employees have formed the nucleus of opposition to deinstitutionalization activities in many states. They argue that the public institutions are in a better position to provide protection and stability for developmentally disabled persons than are private—especially profit-seeking—agencies. Though this agrument obscures the self-interest that employee groups have in perpetuating the institutional system, it is often compelling to parents and others who fear that the developmentally disabled may be prime targets for exploitation.

Fluctuating Accountability

In their haste to decentralize the system of care for developmentally disabled persons by shifting the emphasis away from large, state-run programs, some states have lost their ability to ensure adequate accountability for the well-being of those receiving care. Whereas the institutional system can be scrutinized by the state legislature and citizen groups, small community programs may escape such monitoring. Because many persons have been transferred from institutions to community resources prior to the development of new mechanisms for securing accountability, many states are now faced with the need to devise such mechanisms after the fact.

Love-Hate Relationships with the Private Sector

A major conflict in values concerning the role of the private sector in providing services continues to obstruct the development of resources for the developmentally disabled in many states. Some states have avoided the problem by relying entirely on the public provision of services. But in most states, privately provided care is seen as a necessary evil with at least the capacity to supply services in a more expeditious and efficient manner than the public bureaucracy. And a few states, such as California, have embraced the private sector as the sole provider of service at the community level. In these states, there continues to be a "we-they" dichotomy between the public and private sectors that is reflected in such matters as the setting of rates and standards. This can result in unrealistic cost and programmatic restrictions that may decrease the viability of both the nonprofit and profit-seeking caregivers.

These symptoms of system stress are only some of the general concerns that necessitate a reappraisal of reform efforts and a more integrated vision of implementation in this field.

WHAT NEEDS TO BE DONE

The following pages outline an analytical process that will make it possible for state policymakers to view the entire context in which services for the developmentally disabled are to be restructured. It suggests that the reader inspect both the external and internal imperatives that govern the system before additional decisions are made. It further invites the reader to think through the process of planning during the transition phases from a system dominated by institutional services to one smaller and more responsive to individual needs. Finally, it urges the reader to identify the major functions that, when performed simultaneously, form the core of any successfully integrated complex of services.

Though this book adopts a somewhat academic style, we feel that the risk of seeming overly pretentious is worth taking. This field embodies an extremely complex set of moral, ethical, programmatic, structural, and political issues to which there are clearly no easy answers. Pretending that their resolution is simple is to do disservice to the seriousness of the enterprise. This is not to say that an accommodation cannot be reached. It can, but only after the hard intellectual work has been done.

NOTES

1. The term "developmentally disabled" as used in this book refers to mentally retarded, cerebral palsied, epileptic, learning disabled, autistic, and other similarly disabled individuals as defined by the Developmental Disabled Assistance and Bill of Rights Act of 1975. The issues surrounding deinstitutionalization are most often associated with persons in this group whose developmental problems include mental retardation, however, and this book deals primarily with services to such persons.
2. United States General Accounting Office (GAO), Report to Congress by the Comptroller General of the United States, *Returning the Mentally Disabled to the Community: Government Needs to Do More,* January 7, 1977, p. 9.
3. See: Wolfensberger, W., *Normalization: The Principle of Normalization in Human Services* (Toronto, Canada: National Institute on Mental Retardation, 1972).

4. 42 U.S.C. 2689.
5. Executive Order 11280.
6. See, e.g., *Wyatt v. Stickney,* 344 F.Supp. 373 and 387 (M.S.Ala. 1972), aff'd dub. nom. *Wyatt v. Aderholt,* 503 F.2d 130 (5th Cir. 1974); *New York Association for Retarded Children v. Carey,* 393 F.Supp. (E.D.N.Y. 1975); *Welsh v. Likens,* 373 F.Supp. 487 (D. Minn. 1974), and unreported decision of October 1, 1974; *Pennsylvania Association for Retarded Children v. Pennsylvania,* 344 F.Supp. 1257 (E.D.Pa. 1971) and 343 F.Supp. 279 (E.D.Pa. 1972).
7. This goal was reaffirmed by President Ford in 1974.
8. In 1974, for instance, nursing homes supported by Medicaid funding (Title XIX of the Social Security Act) housed about 2,350, or 26 percent, of the more than 9,000 persons released from 115 public institutions that year (GAO, *op. cit.,* p. 11).

CONTEXT
Chapter two

The process of implementing broad-based reform in the field of care for persons with developmental disabilities should begin with an exploration of the context or environment in which these changes are to take place. This includes the ideological orientation that implicitly or explicitly will guide the development of the system and the more concrete matters related to the current structural organization of the system. This preplanning analysis is essential to an understanding of the potential impact of particular policy options.

For instance, the projected creation of regional fifty-bed community facilities for developmentally disabled persons currently residing in large institutions may run directly counter to a strongly held value among the constituency organizations in the state that asserts that smaller, more "normalizing" living arrangements are not only less stigmatizing but provide a better environment for individual development. Similarly, a course of action that involves the establishment of a network of group homes would of necessity have to be governed by those federal funding arrangements on which the programs would be dependent for reimbursement. Such issues must be faced at the outset or they will very likely come back to haunt state policymakers and administrators when it is perhaps too late to deal with them effectively.

The purpose of this chapter is to help policymakers, administrators, and service providers identify those factors outside of the direct control of the state agency responsible for the administration of services for developmentally disabled persons that set boundaries to any reform activity. These factors are the "givens" in deciding a generally feasible state strategy. They include the normative orientations that are shared by the majority of the program's consumer constituency, the federal and state statutes and regulations that facilitate or constrain service delivery, the major judicial decisions that establish client rights and the range of acceptable program procedures (e.g., individualized treatment planning), and the existing state organizational structure.

EXPLORATION OF VALUES

The first task is to identify the norms or values that are integral parts of any systematic approach to the delivery of services to developmentally disabled persons.[1] The process suggested for the identification of factors that motivate system improvement is essentially deductive. Rather than beginning with the system as it is and inducing strategies and policies that may resolve perceived inadequacies and inefficiencies, it is recommended that generally agreed upon norms or values be identified as a basis for mapping system changes. Clearly, it cannot be a totally deductive process from beginning to end since this would result in a series of "optimal" objectives with questionable chances of success given the practical constraints (e.g., funding and political considerations). It is important, however, to understand what the optimal structure may be before attempting the process of compromise and negotiation essential to the actual implementation of a deinstitutionalization policy.

It is also important to note that values in the field of developmental disabilities are in part a reflection of changing technology and advances in treatment and habilitation. The notion of individualization, for instance, would hardly have been considered thirty years ago, since the state of the art offered few alternatives to custodial, impersonal care. Normalization likewise would have been inconceivable in the absence of evidence that clearly indicates that developmentally disabled persons can be trained to function at higher levels of self care and maintenance. Persons in the field had to raise their own level of expectation before they could understand and accept the value of normalization.

The need to build upon a broader rather than narrower ideological foundation is evidenced in the history of narrowly focused efforts to deinstitutionalize the developmentally disabled. In many ways, the problems that have arisen in past deinstitutionalization efforts are more aptly described as sins of omission rather than commission. They were single-thread approaches that were responsive to a few of the abiding values and goals such as "delivery system efficiency" but less responsive to and even ignorant of others such as "individualization." Thus, even though many of these efforts have been based on a general commitment to provide better programs for such persons, in general they have not been logically deduced from normative principles and have not been conducted in a systematic fashion. As one result, deinstitutionalization has become a highly controversial activity, and there is an increasing clamor for a thorough reassessment of its premises.

person's liberty in order to provide treatment, then, advocates have argued, the state must fulfill its part of the bargain by providing an adequate level of care. Without this *quid pro quo,* commitment becomes a tool for relieving families and communities of their responsibilities.

Where commitment procedures for the mentally retarded are separate from those for the mentally ill, the problem is slightly different. Many states have adopted a "voluntary" admission procedure to be followed when there is no parent or guardian with authority to place an individual in a state or community facility. This process raises questions of consent, since developmentally disabled persons may be more easily coerced than other persons into signing voluntary admission papers. Other advocates have argued that these admissions are never truly voluntary when no alternative living arrangements are available. These issues are particularly significant in those states where voluntary admission presumes that the facility has the right to hold a resident involuntarily for a stipulated period of time (from three to ten days as a rule) if he or she requests release.

Many other facets of state commitment laws have come into question as well, including provisions regarding the right to counsel, the right to a jury trial, the duration of commitment, and periodic review of the need for continuing commitment. In order to meet a constitutional test in any one of these areas, it may be necessary for a state to adopt more formal and complex procedures, but the added short-run costs of doing so may be more than offset by long-run savings resulting from a reduction in inappropriate commitments.[5]

Personal Rights

Recent cases suggest, nevertheless, that civil commitment has been accompanied by significant restrictions on civil rights, including freedom of association and speech, the right to privacy, and the right to protection from harm. Several decisions in such cases have stated that persons being held involuntarily should not be subject to restrictions similar to those placed on criminals, especially in the absence of the same due process guarantees, but this matter has not been decided by the U.S. Supreme Court. Important due process requirements have been included in decisions in several regions of the country, however, and could conceivably be affirmed by the Supreme Court. The Court long ago made clear that where states deny fundamental rights, the constitutionality of the states' actions will be put under "strict scrutiny" for violation of constitutional rights guaranteed by the 14th Amendment.[6]

The central question is: Does the developmentally disabled citizen have the same right of equal protection under law as is guaranteed to other citizens? Some argue that state laws restricting the fundamental rights of developmentally disabled citizens should be subject to the "strict scrutiny" test; that is, the state must prove a "compelling state interest" before it can restrict any rights.

Many advocates of the rights of developmentally disabled persons also argue that this group should be regarded as a "suspect classification" in areas which involve deprivation of rights. If this were the case, it would automatically subject any state law pertaining to the mentally retarded to the "strict scrutiny/compelling state interest" test. Others assert that the state need only prove some "reasonable relation" between the interests it seeks to enhance or protect and a restriction on the rights of developmentally disabled persons. Although the Supreme Court has yet to extend the suspect classification doctrine beyond racial discrimination, it is nevertheless safe to say that the federal courts will not accept a blanket classification of "mentally retarded" as justification for restricting basic personal rights. It is very likely that when the rights of the developmentally disabled are at issue the burden of proof is going to be on the states to show that:

Some restriction of freedom is necessary, either for the protection of the state or the client

The particular restriction chosen is necessary and applicable to the particular client

The means chosen to restrict the freedom will accomplish the stated purposes

There are no less drastic or less restrictive alternatives available that would accomplish the same purpose

Consent

Every individual has the common law right to control his or her person and property. An individual must give voluntary and intelligent concurrence or acquiescence to any action affecting either. When this right is not recognized, as in the case of unlawful trespass or battery (physical abuse), the person responsible can be held liable. For example, if retarded persons are physically abused in public facilities, are treated against their will, or are denied due process in some manner, the responsible state officials may be liable under any number of common law "tort" theories having to do with assault, false imprisonment, intentional infliction of severe emotional distress, and so forth. In addition, state officials may be liable under common law theories of negligence where consent is not an issue (e.g., malpractice).

Where developmentally disabled persons are concerned, matters of consent present particularly thorny problems. Because a determination of what is truly informed consent is difficult to make, activities such as medical intervention, appointment of a guardian, disposal of property, and criminal and civil proceedings are many times problematic when they involve such a person. The courts have shown a willingness to scrutinize such instances very closely to ensure fairness and to eliminate the overreaching of authority, unfair advantage, or the use of coercion. Specific questions of consent raised in recent years relate to sterilization, drug experimentation, and organ donation.

Adequacy of Services

In addition to hearing cases concerning commitment proceedings, guardianship, and consent procedures, state and federal courts have shown a growing disposition in recent years to hear cases concerning the adequacy of services to the developmentally disabled. The premises upon which such cases have been brought to trial have ranged from the traditional matters of cruel and unusual punishment, involuntary servitude, and denial of equal protection to two relatively new "rights": the right to treatment and the right to habilitation.

The landmark case in this area was *Wyatt v. Stickney*. In this case, the district court found that conditions in Alabama's institutions for the mentally retarded were abysmal and that this compromised the facility's ability to provide an acceptable level of care and treatment. The court further found that in the absence of such care and treatment, the *quid pro quo* inherent in the commitment process (care in exchange for liberty) had been violated. The court called this tacit exchange the "right to habilitation."[7] In order to ensure an acceptable level of compliance, the court ordered the state to meet an extensive series of requirements as to physical plant and staffing levels. Most of the standards imposed were those of various professional organizations in the field of care for developmentally disabled persons.

This same approach has characterized the decisions of courts across the country. Whether justified as necessary to implement a right to treatment, a right to habilitation, or a right to freedom from harm, the result of most of the decisions and a larger number of consent decrees has been to implement professionally approved standards for the care and treatment of persons in institutions.[8]

In addition to arguing the right to treatment and habilitation to secure better conditions for the developmentally disabled who reside in institutions, their advocates have also pressed a much older theory—"the least drastic means"—to argue for their clients' right to placement in smaller, more "normal" environments. This concept, now referred to as the "least restrictive alternative," has been described as follows:

> . . . even though the governmental purpose be legitimate and substantial, that purpose cannot be pursued by means that broadly stifle fundamental personal liberties when the end can be more narrowly achieved. The breadth of legislative abridgement must be viewed in the light of less drastic means for achieving the same basic purpose.[9]

Accepted in several leading cases concerning both mental health and mental retardation, the concept has resulted in court orders to move institutional residents to other facilities wherever such facilities exist. According to these decisions, the state has the burden of proving not only that it is accomplishing some legitimate purpose by holding an institutional resident for care and/or treatment, but that the current placement represents the least restrictive setting available to meet the individual's needs.[10]

Though there has been little litigation over standards of care in smaller residential programs, many believe this area will be the next battleground. At least one recent court decision has required that minimum standards be established for the care of children residing in private, out-of-state facilities.[11]

Access to Generic Services

In addition to requiring that developmentally disabled persons receive the care and treatment they need, the courts have acted to see that they receive the benefits of other services as well. For example, several decisions have affirmed a "right to education" for developmentally disabled persons. In what is perhaps the most well known case of this type, the district court for the District of Columbia held that failure to provide mentally retarded children in mental institutions with a free public education constituted a denial of equal protection of the laws.[12] In Pennsylvania, a three-judge district court reached much the same conclusion and permanently enjoined that state from denying free public education on the grounds that a child is uneducable or unable to profit from such education.[13]

More recently, the right to education and other public services has been written into federal law under the provisions of Section 504 of the Rehabilitation Act of 1973. That section, which has been interpreted to cover the mentally retarded as well as other handicapped persons, reads, in part:

> No otherwise qualified handicapped individual in the United States . . . shall solely by reason of his handicap, be excluded from participation in, be denied the benefits of, or be subjected to discrimination under any program or activity receiving Federal financial assistance.

Since all public schools receive federal financial assistance, it is likely that the focus of litigation will now shift to questions about the quality of education provided for the developmentally disabled. Implementation of the "504 regulations" should also give mentally retarded persons clear rights of action to redress wrongs with respect to other municipal and state services, including transportation, housing, welfare, job training, and employment.

Implications for Analysis

The foregoing is not meant to be a comprehensive guide to all of the legal issues affecting developmentally disabled persons. Important differences in state statutes and case law (or the lack thereof) make it impossible to do more in this short space than to suggest the kinds of legal issues administrators and policymakers must take into account. Any administrator who ventures into this field should engage the services of a lawyer specializing in mental disability law. Once the legal issues in a particular state have been identified, the next step is to analyze their ramifications and to develop specific plans that will ensure compliance and reduce the possibility of unnecessary litigation.

Although each state policymaker and administrator must develop courses of action specific to the circumstances in his or her state, the following are examples of steps that might be taken to improve care and reduce the chance of litigation:

Where funds are scarce, it is important to develop those aspects of client habilitation that will have the maximum impact on individual client dignity and that, therefore, may have more credibility with the courts. Such improvements could include participation of residents in the habilitation planning process, provision of individual storage space, reduced use of institutionalized clothing, more organized use of volunteers, etc.

Because of the time pressures placed on institutional managers and the difficulty that any administrator has in being objective about his or her program, it is suggested that outside, multidisciplinary audit teams be brought into institutions periodically to examine compliance with patients' rights requirements. Such audits may serve as "early warning" systems to signal breaches that could become causes for litigation.

Many legal problems arise from insufficient financial support. Consumer groups, the governor's staff, professional organizations, and state legislators must be made aware of the potential consequences of inadequate funding. Identification of and work with one or more state legislators who take a special interest in the developmentally disabled is particularly advisable. By supplying these legislators with useful information about the program, consulting them on key management decisions, and asking for their assistance in the evaluation of system performance, the administrator can ensure the development of expertise and support in the legislative body.

Administrators should actively encourage and participate in the development of independent client advocacy systems. This will not only demonstrate openness on the part of the administration but also makes it easier to achieve the ends that both advocates and professionals seek with regard to the welfare of developmentally disabled persons. Client advocates can also help to keep down inappropriate admissions and ensure that only those who have no better alternative are admitted to state institutions.

State officials should ensure that the judiciary in their state and region is fully informed regarding the practical problems inherent in the reform of institutional programs. For example, they should know that problems in recruitment of trained manpower and the retraining of existing staff may significantly delay the implementation of complex court orders.

Administrators who favor community-based care may find themselves as the defendants in litigation brought by those who seek to upgrade care for the developmentally disabled. This has occurred in Massachusetts and other states and points out the necessity of maintaining administrative flexibility at certain junctures in the consent decree. Unless, for instance, "least restrictive alternative" provisions are included in the standards of the decree, officials run the risk of providing expensive institutional improvements without the authority to reduce institutional populations.

Though there is no single set of answers to the problems of litigation, the foregoing should suggest the types of steps that might be taken to avoid lengthy suits. The key in developing such strategies is to realize that, in most cases, litigation is meant to improve state programs and not as a personal attack on individual administrators. The administrator who views legal intervention as a possible aid to his or her own work and who shows a willingness to cooperate with legal advocates is likely to be more successful than the administrator who doggedly resents and resists litigation and the development of mental disability case law.

ORGANIZATIONAL STRUCTURE

Every state has developed its own political and organizational structures based on its cultural, geographic, and demographic characteristics. It is important, therefore, that state officials concerned about improving care for disabled persons assess the broad organizational context in which reform is to be carried out and the extent to which important elements are rooted in history or tradition and therefore difficult to change.

For instance, in the early 1970s Georgia attempted to establish a regional human services network to coordinate all state-financed programs at the local level. Although the concept could not be faulted, it totally ignored the traditional power and authority of the local health officers. They and their supporters eventually forced the state to abandon the enterprise, and the system reverted to its original structure. This particular organizational reality should not have been ignored, and if strategies had been developed to work within the system some compromise might have been achieved.

Relationships among the various organizational elements must also be assessed. These include the relationships between the lead agency responsible for services to developmentally disabled persons and local service providers, the lead agency and other state human services agencies, the lead agency and the Developmental Disabilities Council, and so forth. The initial assessment should be an attempt to catalogue and perhaps graphically describe existing relationships and structures to determine which are likely to be enduring and endemic to the state and which can be altered without damage to the fabric and efficacy of the program. Finally, state officials must consider the changes that are necessary within the organizational structure to make it more responsive to the needs of developmentally disabled persons. Guidelines for such decisions are provided in Chapter IV.

State officials may be aided in developing an understanding of their own state organizational structure by the following brief descriptions of the major models that prevail throughout the country at the state and local level.

State Developmental Disabilities Authorities

The term "Developmental Disabilities Authority" (DDA) is used to describe that entity at the state level that has responsibility for overseeing the provision of public services to developmentally disabled persons and therefore has a direct interest in deinstitutionalization and the development of community alternatives. Many of the state agencies that are included under this rubric are not technically responsible for the full range of programs for developmentally disabled persons but are legally mandated only to provide services to the mentally retarded. In the majority of cases, however, the mental retardation agency does have *de facto* responsibility for other developmentally disabled persons, especially when their disabilities are associated with mental retardation or their handicaps are sufficiently disabling that they require habilitative, residential, or other services. Although this is not totally satisfactory (e.g., autistic or learning-disabled persons may relate to agencies other than the mental retardation agency), it is the most useful focus for this analysis.

In characterizing the distinctions among DDAs, the terms "substantial," "partial," "line," and "no line" authority are used to describe the operational relationships that the DDA has with the delivery system. "Substantial line authority" is defined to include the power to make some or all of the operational decisions that affect or alter the conduct of the system functions described in Chapter IV. "Partial" and "no line" authority mean little or no direct responsibility for carrying out the function outlined. It is assumed that DDAs with little or no line authority maintain staff relationships with supervising agencies or personnel who act on recommendations for action from the DDA. The three basic categories are:

Autonomous agencies These are state DDAs that operate as separate state departments or agencies and have substantial line authority over community-based and institutional programs (Illinois).

Agencies within a department of mental health These are DDAs that function as divisions or agencies within departments of mental health. In most instances such departments are required by state statutes or regulations to be directed by a psychiatrist. Two general administrative models exist within this category. One consists of DDAs with substantial line authority for community-based and institutional programs (Massachusetts). The other consists of DDAs with partial or no line authority (Virginia).

Agencies within umbrella departments These are DDAs that function as components of a combined health and/or human services department. Two categories also exist under this model. One consists of DDAs with substantial line authority for community-based and institutional care (Maryland). The other consists of DDAs with partial or no line authority (Pennsylvania).

It should be noted that the formal organizational structure does not always reflect the informal exercise of power within a bureaucracy. Therefore, no model of this type is ever truly predictive or descriptive of actual practice. This construct does, however, point out major functional differences that can guide an analysis of a state system. For instance, in order to implement single-stream funding for developmental disabilities services, those DDAs that currently have no line authority over the budgeting process for institutions or community-based services would require significant reorganization either through executive order or statutory change. Additionally, if new standards are required for the development of community residential services in a state where the DDA has no regulatory authority in that area, reorganization or the assignment of such responsibility to the appropriate operational entity would be required.

State Developmental Disabilities Councils

State Developmental Disabilities (DD) Councils vary greatly in the amount of power that they are capable of exercising, the position that they occupy in the state structure, and the independent staff resources that they are able to call upon.

Clearly, all DD Councils have those minimum powers as defined by the federal Developmental Disabilities Act, including authority to create a plan, allocate funds, identify service needs, and coordinate state agencies on behalf of developmentally disabled persons. With respect to these powers and responsibilities, however, the General Accounting Office, in its five-state investigation of deinstitutionalization, has recently commented that the DD Councils have shown little ability to influence the delivery system to the extent anticipated by the Act.[14] State officials should determine whether or not the viability of the councils is related to their position within the bureaucracy or to other variables mentioned.

Table 2-1 displays the different variables that ought to be taken into account in categorizing state DD Councils in terms of location in the bureaucracy, statutory powers, and staff resources.

Local Organizations

Although all states have at some point in their history established state-run institutions to care for persons with developmental disabilities, the structure of local, community-based services varies greatly. The major categories of financing and organization include:

State grants-in-aid Under this model, the state appropriates specific funds for the provision of grants to local provider agencies. Such grants are usually based on recommendations from state regional agencies or local citizen's groups (Massachusetts).

Locally based services This method of service delivery usually occurs in states where there is a strong history of local control and the provision of human and health services by local governing bodies. Under this arrangement, states and localities enter a partnership in which they share in the costs of

Table 2-1. Powers and resources of state Developmental Disabilities Councils*

Location	Council's powers: Additional powers granted by state statute	Council's powers: No additional state statutory powers	Staff: Independent	Staff: Provided by parent agency
Governor's Office				
Human Services Agency	X		X	
DDA				
Autonomous				

* In this case, California is used as an example.

services. The local governing body, usually guided by an appointed citizen's board, prepares the budget and plans for services, and submits it to the DDA (or other agency) for review and approval (Pennsylvania and Virginia).

Regional nonprofit agencies and purchase of services Under this model, the state DDA contracts with regional, private nonprofit entities for the provision of diagnostic and evaluation services. In addition, each regional "center" is given a budget for the purchase of services on behalf of its developmentally disabled clients. The centers, in conjunction with regional citizen's boards, prepare budgets and plans for their areas, and those budgets and plans are then submitted to the state DDA (California).

Regional nonprofit agencies providing direct service This model is similar to the one above except that the regional nonprofit entities provide direct services to their clients in addition to diagnosis and evaluation. Thus, for example, house parents of group homes may be staff of the regional structure rather than personnel of other nonprofit or proprietary agencies (ENCOR, Nebraska).

Regional, state-run service centers Such centers are similar to the two described above except that the regional diagnostic unit is operated by the state. Such centers may or may not operate direct services (Illinois).

Institutional based centers Some states have opted to utilize existing state-run residential institutions as the focal point for the organization and delivery of services at the local level (Florida).

Regional human services centers Some states have experimented with the provision of direct services to developmentally disabled persons through regional human services agencies. Though still in the experimental stages, this model is definitely one that should be considered in any overall design (Delaware).

Undoubtedly, there are other variations on the theme, but these categories should exhaust the major constellations. Again, the assessment or creation of any one of these forms of service delivery must be done with an understanding of the unique social and political context in which it must operate.

FEDERAL FUNDING

Although the creation and support of services for developmentally disabled persons are essentially state responsibilitities, the major federal health, social welfare, and employment programs play a substantial role in individual client support and the generation of resources. These federal programs can support state efforts to reform services, but their attendant restrictions and regulations can also compromise or alter desired programmatic changes.

Many state officials have become discouraged in attempting to sort out the positive and negative aspects of federal aid and in developing strategies for the utilization of that aid. Among the reasons are:

The considerable time and effort (cost) involved in determining and repeatedly verifying individual eligibility

The loss of state and local autonomy resulting from rigid federal requirements

The short-term nature and somewhat uncertain future of many of the federal funding programs

The inappropriateness and ineffectiveness of services organized primarily in response to federal funding requirements rather than to the needs of the developmentally disabled persons to be served

Federal laws and guidelines can have a significant effect on state planning and the operation of services for developmentally disabled persons. A good example is the impact that the new standards for Intermediate Care Facilities for the Mentally

Retarded (ICF/MR) has had on particular states. Promulgated in 1974, the standards were due to be fully operational in March of 1977. Though this deadline has been moved ahead, the prospect of the eventual enforcement of these standards has forced many states, including California, Massachusetts, Georgia, and Connecticut, to reassess current institutional populations. They are doing so to determine which residents can be moved into the community in order to decrease the amount of capital improvements that will be required to bring existing institutions up to the new standards.

The ICF/MR standards have also forced states to consider the immediate and long-term implications that these requirements will have for Medicaid revenues and to explore a variety of other funding arrangements that might be utilized to support clients in the community. In those states that have systematically responded to the challenge presented by the new regulations, more creative funding and program patterns may emerge. In other words, it is within the power of many state officials to turn what may have appeared to be adversity into an opportunity for systems growth and change.

Failure to be attentive to the snares and benefits presented by federal programs, however, may result in a "stunted" system for the delivery of services to developmentally disabled persons. It can lead to an over-reliance on one mode of financing to the exclusion of all others. This can jeopardize the stability of the system and make it vulnerable to the shifting objectives of particular federal policies. The ICF/MR issue is again a case in point. Those states that moved rapidly to qualify as many programs as possible under the original ICF program are now faced with the potential loss of thousands of dollars unless the new compliance standards are met.

If state officials do not master the use and exigencies of federal resources, the federal regulations may tend to dominate the conduct of state systems. To avoid this, state policymakers and administrators must survey all funding possibilities, select those that are consistent with state objectives, and maintain a financial base that is sufficiently flexible to withstand periodic changes in federal policies.

Characteristics of the Principal Federal Programs

There are a myriad of federal programs that in one way or another can provide support for services to developmentally disabled persons.[16] The key to selecting those with the most direct impact is in first determining the shape and content of the services to be provided rather than allowing this conception to be governed by the requirements of a particular funding source. This will help to ensure continuity of resource development and will prevent the all too frequent "client following the funds" dilemma.

In selecting the types of federal resources that will be utilized, each program should be assessed to determine eligibility standards, funding levels, and advantages and disadvantages to the state. To provide a sample of the way in which this initial exploration might proceed, seven major federal programs are described briefly in the appendix at the end of this chapter. This description is neither definitive nor exhaustive, of course, but it does illustrate the type of analysis that should be conducted. Since it represents only some of the federal programs that should be evaluated as part of a comprehensive campaign to develop resources for developmentally disabled persons, the reader should become familiar with other important programs, for example, Child Welfare (Title IV-B of the Social Security Act), Maternal and Child Health (Title V of the Social Security Act), Section 202 construction funds from the Department of Housing and Urban Development (HUD), Community Development Block Grants, and revenue sharing.

Development of Specific State Strategies

Once an evaluation of relevant federal programs has been conducted, state officials should proceed to create short- and long-term federal funding strategies tailored to the particular state context. The following are some brief examples of the ways in which some states have adapted particular federal programs to their needs.

Title XVI (Supplemental Security Income) (SSI) New York and many other states have established variable SSI supplemental payments depending on the level of care and supervision required by the SSI eligible client. This state payment is in addition to the basic federal monthly SSI payment of $177.80. In Pennsylvania's domiciliary care program for adults, each eligible individual receives a supplement of $147.30, which assures the recipient of a monthly income of $325.10. A domiciliary care home in Pennsylvania can accommodate no more than thirteen clients and must be certified by an approved placement agency.

Title XIX (Medicaid) Although many states have not used the ICF/MR program to stimulate smaller residences, Minnesota is currently operating a "fifteen bed or less" program for developmentally disabled clients under a test case agreement with the Department of Health, Education, and Welfare's (HEW) Office of Long Term Care in Region V. Massachusetts has proposed to HEW that it be allowed to use ICF/MR funds for a "conglomerate" of small satellite living areas. It is hoped that this approach will demonstrate alternative ways in which ICF/MR services can be delivered to promote more normalizing and supportive community living arrangements. Instead of large institutional settings, Massachusetts is proposing to establish a number of alternative service delivery modes that can provide greater flexibility in implementing individual service plans. All six models discussed by Massachusetts provide the mandatory ICF/MR services even though the focus of responsibility for delivery of mandated services is different in each model.

Vocational Rehabilitation The California Department of Rehabilitation is attempting to overcome unfamiliarity with problems of the developmentally disabled on the part of counselors by taking two important steps: (1) developmental disabilities specialists have been placed in each of its substate offices in order to train generic counselors, and (2) in conjunction with the California Department of Health, the Department has developed a project to expand the skills of staff working in training programs for developmentally disabled clients in the newest methods of skill development. Other vocational rehabilitation agencies are developing similar cooperative agency agreements to promote the community support needs of the developmentally disabled. Area rehabilitation agencies in Indiana have coordinated their diagnostic evaluations, training programs, and job placement services with appropriate residential and social service agencies.

Title XX Initially, the State of Nebraska was very successful in combining state and local dollars to match federal Title XX funds to support numerous community support activities. Severe cutbacks were made in fiscal years 1975 and 1976, however, when the state ceiling was reached.

Title XX is being used in Massachusetts to fund community residential services, case management, sheltered workshops, day care activity centers, and therapeutic day care for developmentally disabled individuals. Recently, the University of Massachusetts obtained a federal grant to develop the use of Title XX training funds for state hospital employees who may lose their jobs as a result of deinstitutionalization.

South Carolina's Department of Mental Retardation (DMR) has taken advantage of Title XX training funds by contracting with a "university-affiliated facility" to train employees of local community agencies that provide DMR contractual services to eligible Title XX clients. The areas of training include individual assessment and program planning, client goal setting, recreation, evaluation, institutional methods, and normalization.

Section 8 (HUD Rent Subsidies) Massachusetts and some other states are urging their vendors to assist clients in applying for Section 8 aid and are pursuing needed regulatory changes in the Section 8 program. Other states, including Virginia, Minnesota, Michigan, and New Jersey, have negotiated with their state housing finance development agency or their community affairs agency to set aside a percentage of their Section 8 allocations for the developmentally disabled. In some of these states, state support has been added to stimulate the construction or rehabilitation of group homes to be occupied by Section 8 clients.

Developmental Disabilities Act A creative example of how one state used Developmental Disabilities monies to "free-up" scarce state funds may be found in New Jersey. The New Jersey DD Council awarded a grant to the state's Department of Community Affairs to help meet the housing needs of the mentally retarded and physically handicapped. As a result, an extensive housing program for the handicapped was developed which included, among other things, the leasing of 410 Section 8 units in four New Jersey counties. Ohio and other states have provided numerous awards to public and private agencies for the development of residential programs. In Massachusetts, such funds have been used to assist potential providers of residential services to carry out capital improvements necessary to meet specific fire and life safety standards.

NOTES

1. Braddock refers to this as the "ideology or belief system which suggests models for delivering services." See David Braddock, *Opening Closed Doors: The Deinstitutionalization of Disabled Individuals* (Reston, Virginia: Council for Exceptional Children, 1977), p. 3.
2. *Wyatt v. Stickney,* 344 F.Supp. 373 and 387 (M.D. Ala. 1972 aff'd sub. nom.), *Wyatt v. Aderholt,* 503 F.2d 1305 (5th Cir. 1974).

2a. *N.Y. Association for Retarded Children and Parisi v. Carey* 393 F. Supp. (E.D.N.Y. 1975).

2b. *Wyatt v. Stickney, op. cit.*
3. See Appendix II for a list of prominent case citations.
4. *Jackson v. Indiana,* 406 U.S. 715 (1974), and *O'Connor v. Donaldson,* 422 U.S. 563 (1975), decided in 1974 and mid-1975, were the first major modern Supreme Court decisons in the area of mental health and mental retardation. Both cases have narrow holdings that limit their value in providing national benchmarks.
5. Specific federal court decisions and standards in the area of civil commitment and the other three areas discussed here are included in Appendix II.
6. The Supreme Court long ago made clear that where states deny fundamental rights, the constitutionality of the states' actions will be put under "strict scrutiny" for violation of constitutional rights guaranteed by the 14th Amendment.
7. The court defined this term, "right to habilitation," as "the process by which the staff of the institution assists the resident to acquire and maintain those skills which enable him to cope more effectively with the demands of his own person and of his environment and to raise the level of his physical, mental and social efficiency. Habilitation includes but is not limited to programs of formal, structured education and treatment."
8. *Wyatt v. Stickney, op.cit.; NYARC and Parisi v. Carey, op. cit.; Welsch v. Likens,* 373 F.Supp. 487 (D.Minn. 1974); *Horachek v. Exxon,* 357 F.Supp. 71 (D.Neb. 1973); *Davis v. Watkins,* 384 F.Supp. 1196 (N.D.Ohio 1974); *Ricci v. Greenblatt,* Civil No. 72-469 (D.Mass. 1972); *Nathan v. Levitt,* No. 74 Ch. 4080 (Cir. Ct., Cook Co., Ill.), Consent order 3/26/76; *Gross v. State of Hawaii,* Civ. Action No. 43090 (Cir. Ct. Ha.), Consent decree 2/3/76; *Rouse v. Cameron,* 373 F.2d 451 (D.C. Cir. 1966); *Patients v. Camden County Board of Freeholders,* N.L. 33417-74 PW (N.J. Super. Ct.) 5/19 and 10/12/76.
9. *Shelton v. Tucker,* 364 U.S. 479, 488 (1960).
10. Cases which have required states to place patients in less restrictive alternatives include *Wyatt v. Stickney, op.cit.; Welsch v. Likens, op.cit.; Dixon v. Weinberger,* 405 F.Supp. 974 (D.D.C. 1975); *Lessard v. Schmidt,* 349 F.Supp. 1078 (E.D.Wisc. 1972); *Lake v. Cameron,* 364 F.2d 657 (D.C.Cir. 1966); *Dixon v. Attorney General,* 325 F.Supp. 966 (M.D.Pa. 1971).
11. *Gary v. State of Louisiana,* Civil No. 74-2412 (D.La. 1976).
12. *Mills v. Board of Education,* 348 F.Supp. 866 (D.D.C. 1972).
13. *PARC v. Pennsylvania,* 343 F.Supp. 279 (E.D.Pa. 1972).
14. GAO, *op.cit.*
15. Some of the material for this section was taken from: President's Committee on Mental Retardation, *Mental Retardation Trends in State Services* (Washington, D.C.: U.S. Government Printing Office, 1976).
16. For an extensive listing, see U.S. Department of Health, Education, and Welfare, Office of the Assistant Secretary for Human Development, Office for Handicapped Individuals, *Federal Assistance for Programs Serving the Handicapped,* 76-22001.

APPENDIX: SEVEN MAJOR FEDERAL PROGRAMS THAT PROVIDE FINANCIAL SUPPORT

Federal program	Basic facts	Analysis of constraints
Title XVI, Social Security Act—Supplemental Security Income (SSI)	Title XVI provides a monthly support allowance for indigent disabled, blind, and aged individuals who meet certain income and disability criteria. The maximum federal payment is currently set at $177.80 per month but can be supplemented by states. The federal government will administer the state supplement as well as the federal payments if a state wishes. If an eligible SSI client is residing in a state medical institution or nursing home, an intermediate care facility, etc., that is receiving "substantial" Medicaid reimbursement, such person is entitled to $25 per month for personal expenses. All SSI clients are eligible for Medicaid, social services, and food stamps and must be referred to Vocational Rehabilitation if they are deemed potentially employable. If they are accepted for Vocational Rehabilitation, they are required to participate in the program or risk losing benefits. A series of recent amendments removed several restrictive provisions that prevented the utilization of SSI by potential clients and added new protections for recipients.	With respect to restrictions on the use of SSI for residents in publicly operated residences with sixteen beds or less, SSI has tentatively ruled that the *total* number of SSI recipients living in an apartment house must be taken into account when such residences are operated by a single agency. Additionally, computation of unearned income poses problems. Though state and local assistance based on need is excluded, the federal government has defined "need" to be economic and thus excludes social needs. This may mean the denial of benefits to thousands of disabled individuals. Other restrictions include: (1) a one-third reduction in benefits if a recipient lives in the household of another person; (2) a recipient's earnings are counted against him or her if the recipient is in a "trial" employment period of up to twelve months, unless the earnings are part of a plan for self-support; (3) for severely disabled persons, the trial work period reviewed at nine months and terminated at twelve months may not be long enough to test sufficiently the viability of the client's work skills; (4) once the trial work period is terminated automatic

Among the changes were: (1) residents of publicly operated facilities housing sixteen or fewer clients can now receive SSI payments; (2) the provision of certain state-supported services can no longer be translated into unearned income and deducted from an individual's SSI payment; (3) SSI payments will not be reduced if the facility in which an SSI recipient resides provides services that could be covered under Medicaid; and (4) states must designate state and local authorities to establish and enforce standards for any type of institution (foster homes and group homes) in which a significant number of SSI recipients reside. Standards for SSI facilities will be incorporated in state Title XX plans and made available for public review. If group care facilities are not approved by the standard setting authorities, the federal SSI payment will be reduced; and (5) all SSI-eligible children will now be referred to the State Crippled Children's agency or other designated agency instead of the Vocational Rehabilitation agency, as previously required.

benefits such as Medicaid also cease; (5) payments made by parents can also reduce the SSI benefit; and (6) long delays in processing SSI for disabled persons may cause hardships for those without presumptive disabilities.

Title XIX, Social Security Act—Medicaid

In any state Medicaid Program, the federal share is never less than 50 percent and can be as high as 83 percent, depending on the state's poverty index and population base.

Utilization of Title XIX funds for ICF/MRs requires compliance with a variety of federal and state fire and life safety codes and may limit the types of clients that can

continued

Federal program	Basic facts	Analysis of constraints
Title XIX (continued)	There are three principal ways in which Medicaid can support the developmentally disabled: (1) through institutional programs, (2) through the delivery of general medical care, and (3) through the provision of therapeutic rehabilitative services. Noninstitutional Medicaid programs provide medical and other health-related services to low income persons either on an outpatient or inpatient basis. Five types of medical services must be provided by the state including inpatient, outpatient, laboratory and x-ray, skilled nursing for individuals twenty-one years and over, and physician services. Additional programs including day care, dental services, physical therapy, and occupational therapy can be funded at the option of the state. Home health care was an optional service until July 1, 1970, but the states are now required to provide such care. Regulations published on August 26, 1976, require all states to provide: (1) nursing, (2) home health aides, and (3) medical supplies, equipment, and appliances as part of their home health program. States cannot require that home health benefits be contingent on	be served (i.e., to more ambulatory and higher functioning developmentally disabled persons). Because of these requirements, it may be difficult to encourage the creation of smaller facilities, given the economies of scale. Additionally, depending on the size of proposed ICF/MR facilities, the regional health services agency may have to give its approval to the project. Any optional medical services for the developmentally disabled, such as dental care, must be approved by the state legislature, since it is up to this body to raise state matching funds. Other problems include the establishment of rates of reimbursement to adequately support a residential program and the mobilization of required ICF/MR services (dentistry, record-keeping, medical oversight) for small group settings. Given all the "institutional" requirements that still exist under ICF/MR, the development of small facilities under this program is extremely costly. Finally, many states may have to spend substantial sums to bring existing facilities up to ICF/MR standards. This investment will more than likely improve the quality of care in the institutions; however, it will also

discharge from any type of hospital or institution (as is the case in Medicare). Institutional programs such as skilled nursing facilities and intermediate care facilities are supported in large part by Medicaid. For the developmentally disabled, creation of a separate ICF/MR funding category has resulted in extensive new requirements and standards that must be met in the forthcoming years.

Current ICF/MR regulations allow the use of funds for residences with fifteen beds or less. In such cases, instead of applying the institutional requirements of the Life Safety Code, the section of the Code dealing with lodging or rooming houses can be applied in cases where residents are ambulatory and capable of self preservation. A modified nursing personnel requirement can also be applied to these residences.

Other facets of the program that facilitate resource development include provisions allowing states to continue to bill Medicaid (through the end of the appropriate fiscal year) for beds vacated by residents moved into community programs, and a provision encouraging demonstration projects to test the feasibility of prospective reimbursement schemes. substantially increase the state's investment in and commitment to institutional services at the expense of its community-based service network.

HEW has recently contracted with the National Bureau of Standards to study the possibility of expanding these regulations for those developmentally disabled persons who are incapable of self preservation.

continued

Federal program	Basic facts	Analysis of constraints
Title XX, Social Security Act—Social Services	Title XX funds are allocated to states on a formula grant basis with the federal government reimbursing states for 75 percent of social service costs. Private, state, and local funds can be used as match. Although Title XX is currently operating under a $2.5 billion ceiling, funds for training and retraining of social services personnel are available outside of the ceiling. A bill currently pending in Congress would raise the ceiling to $2.7 billion. If the Title XX agency so provides in its annual plan, funds can be used for a range of community support services including resocialization programs, protective services, recreational programs, and transportation. Title XX can also fund temporary room or board costs in emergency situations or for up to six months when such residential placement is a subordinate but integral part of the service plan. Since Title XX is a modified "revenue-sharing" approach to the delivery of social services, the ultimate decision as to what services are provided, and to whom, lies with the state agency designated to receive this aid. There are, however, three general requirements imposed on the states by the federal government: (1) the services pro-	The current Title XX funding ceiling is inadequate, and most states have reached it or soon will. As a result, few states have been able to implement new services with this aid. Second, because this program covers many disadvantaged groups, the planning process may become political and volatile. As a result, there may be little or no continuity in the delivery of a particular service from year to year. Third, reimbursement under Title XX is not only very slow (six to nine months), but the rates are often set too low to cover actual operating costs. Fourth, if state income limits are set too high, the needs of very low income clients may be neglected; but if the limits are set too low, many lower-middle income developmentally disabled individuals and their families will not be eligible. For example, for any child-oriented service, the family's income is considered as part of the child's income, and often the children are precluded from receiving services because of the income status of their families. Fifth, training funds are difficult to secure and are not available for the retraining of personnel on institutional payrolls. Only $60 million was expended for this purpose in fiscal year 1975–1976.

vided must be directed at five program goals, two of which concern self support and the prevention of inappropriate institutional care; (2) three of the social services must be made available to all SSI recipients; and (3) 50 percent of all funds must be used for services to Aid to Families with Dependent Children (AFDC), SSI, or Medicaid recipients. In addition to these "categorically needy persons," services can also be provided to persons with incomes between 80 percent and 115 percent of a state's median income. However, fees must be charged according to a sliding scale for this group of individuals.

Other related drawbacks include: a lack of minimum standards to help ensure consistency and quality among service providers, a lack of accountability measures for Title XX provider agencies, insufficient attention to the assessment of client needs and demands in state planning, and inconsistent interpretation of regulations.

Section 8 HUD Rent Subsidy Programs for Existing, New, and Rehabilitated Housing

The most accessible HUD program for the support of residential services for developmentally disabled clients is the Section 8 Housing Assistance Payment Program. An individual who is disabled, as defined in the Developmental Disabilities Act, or handicapped and can meet certain income requirements can qualify for a HUD rental assistance payment. Eligible clients must contribute at least 15 percent but not more than 25 percent of their total income to the rent. HUD will pay the difference between the client's required contribution and the established rent for the housing unit. Any

There are several constraints within the Section 8 program: (1) Section 8 appropriations fall short of the demand in many communities, and housing for developmentally disabled clients may not be a priority; (2) in some areas, HUD's Fair Market Rents are too low to reflect the actual cost of living and thus do not permit clients to find appropriate and reasonable units; (3) minimum property standards for construction are overly restrictive and unresponsive to small specialized group living arrangements; (4) recipients of this aid frequently become entangled in time-consuming and often frus-

continued

Federal program	Basic facts	Analysis of constraints
Section 8 (continued)	available and approved housing unit that falls within HUD's Fair Market Rents can be used under Section 8. Also, as a result of a recent amendment to the provisions of the Social Security Act (Title XVI) the requirement that HUD rental assistance payments be counted as unearned income has been eliminated. Finally, HUD has proposed regulations to clarify the status of persons living in group facilities housing fewer than sixteen individuals including support personnel such as house parents. These regulations would modify existing housing quality standards such as the one bathroom per resident requirement.	trating negotiations with the public housing authority and landlords; and (5) the proposed regulations for group living still pose problems in Fair Market Rent determinations.
Developmental Disabilities Act (as amended by PL 94-103)	Under the Federal Developmental Disabilities program, grants are made to states for planning and administering services, developing advocacy strategies, and constructing facilities for the developmentally disabled. The federal share may be as high as 75 percent of costs (up to 90 percent in poverty areas) with state, local, or nonprofit organizations providing the remaining funds. The Developmental Disabilities Act is the only piece of federal legislation that specifically requires states to	There are two major drawbacks to the Developmental Disabilities program: (1) the level of funding is inadequate to accomplish the required goals, including the development of an adequate advocacy system to meet the federal regulations; and (2) although a certain percentage of Developmental Disabilities funds can be used for start-up costs, they are not enough to cover continuing capital and operating expenses for facilities. In addition, there is no continuity of service delivery if such short-term

prepare a deinstitutionalization plan for developmentally disabled clients. Other federal programs such as Title XX have deinstitutionalization as a goal but do not require a comprehensive plan for this target group.

funds are used as the primary source of financing. Because there is so little Developmental Disabilities money available, it may be more advantageous for state agencies to use such funds as the "glue" for other related programs and planning processes.

Vocational Rehabilitation Act

Under a complex formula grant allocation, federal funds cover 80 percent of Vocational Rehabilitation service costs while states provide the remaining 20 percent. For SSI clients, however, the federal government will pay 100 percent of Vocational Rehabilitation evaluation and service costs for recipients accepted into the program through a separate allocation (SSI/SSDI).

Amendments to the Vocational Rehabilitation Act in 1974 require that the states give priority to the severely disabled. Other eligible individuals include those with physical or mental disabilities that prevent them from working but who could be employable with the aid of Vocational Rehabilitation services. A variety of support services ranging from diagnosis and counseling to transportation and maintenance during rehabilitation can be covered by Vocational Rehabilitation funds.

Federal law requires state agencies to serve the severely disabled, but criteria for admission to the Vocational Rehabilitation program emphasize the recipient's potential for employment, which may be an unrealistic goal for some developmentally disabled persons. Since Vocational Rehabilitation is also a time-limited program, benefits are limited to those clients who can assimilate more rapidly into the job market. Although the evaluation period can run as long as eighteen months, counselors rarely allow this much time per case. Attempts to include "independent living" as a goal for the more severely disabled have so far been unsuccessful.

Although 100 percent federal funding is available to evaluate and rehabilitate SSI recipients, these funds can only be expended if training will result in a savings to the SSI program and the Vocational Rehabilitation trust fund and the client will

continued

Federal program	Basic facts	Analysis of constraints
Vocational Rehabilitation Act (continued)		be placed in "substantial gainful employment" (i.e., earning $200 per month). This appears to be very restrictive since even in the regular Vocational Rehabilitation program a person who makes one-half the minimum wage is counted as a "successful" placement. Most increases in appropriations for the Vocational Rehabilitation program since 1973, when the severely disabled were first included in the legislation, have been absorbed by inflation. If the priority for serving the severely disabled continues, fewer persons will be able to receive services because it will take longer for them to be trained at a greater cost. As for work opportunities, few options are available outside of sheltered workshops for the severely disabled. Not many developmentally disabled go on to remunerative work from rehabilitation agencies. Yet work opportunities could certainly be expanded with the help of improved technology and more emphasis on rehabilitation in this area. And, finally, there is still the issue of case closures as a performance standard for Vocational Rehabilitation agencies. This

problem is sometimes referred to as "the numbers game." Although HEW has tried to develop a "weighted closure system" for over ten years, no such system has yet been agreed upon.

Education for All Handicapped Children Act (PL 94-142) and the Elementary and Secondary Education Act (PL 89-313)

PL 94-142, the new Education for All Handicapped Children Act, provides federal support for the provision of educational services in programs and facilities that are as nearly "normal" as possible. PL 94-142 also mandates that all states must have a "policy" that guarantees a free appropriate education to every handicapped student from birth to age twenty-one (by September 1978 for children three to eighteen years and September 1980 for children three to twenty years). Other services such as transportation, developmental, corrective, or supportive services must also be provided for those children that need such assistance in order to benefit from special education.

All services must be provided in the least restrictive environment: that is, wherever possible services are to be integrated into a "normal" learning setting. State education agencies will receive PL 94-142 funds up through fiscal year 1977; but in fiscal year 1978, 75 percent of the federal funds will be allocated to local educational agencies.

There are two potential problems that may affect the overlap between PL 94-142 and previous federal education assistance programs—PL 89-313 in particular. Because it is anticipated that all educational programs for developmentally disabled children will be merged into PL 94-142 eventually, some gains from the PL 89-313 provisions may be lost.

The two laws have very different funding formulas, and if they are combined, developmentally disabled children, and especially those in institutions, may suffer. In other words, if PL 94-142 prevails, substantial funding may be withdrawn from educational programs in state facilities.

In addition, both PL 89-313 and PL 94-142 require that noneducational services (room and board, etc.) be provided without cost to a child's parents or guardians. Since most states charge some fees for public residential care, this provision will be in direct conflict with those states' parental liability statutes.

PLANS
Chapter three

CRITICAL CHOICES

The preceding chapter describes the overall context in which planning for reform of the public system of services for developmentally disabled persons does and will take place. The first portion of the discussion lists the general values and norms that form the increasing consensual basis on which improvement of the system is premised. The second part characterizes the concrete external realities that are faced by planners and policymakers in this field.

With respect to the first area—values—the moral and constitutional principles discussed represent the broad aims of any system of services for developmentally disabled persons. They are ultimate ends toward which the system is directed. They form the basis for practice and hold out the promise of more decent treatment of individual developmentally disabled consumers. Their mere espousal in a state plan, however, is not sufficient to guarantee systematic change and improvement. Too many state plans, including those submitted under the Developmental Disabilities Act, are simply recitations of ends derived from these values and are not, therefore, "instruments" with which to accomplish necessary change. Merely to state that services will be premised on a "maximization of individual potential" without articulating the complex system modifications that will be necessary to move toward that end is to substitute rhetoric for systematic thinking.

What must emerge from an acceptance of these guiding principles is a mechanism for achieving an efficient and effective transition from a system built around custodial institutions to one that is integrated into the community and that entails a richer array of service options to meet individual needs. The plan, then, must be a new creation—one that is motivated by the principles described but that also sets out concrete choices based on the particular reality of a state's resources, culture, politics, and history. No plan, given the special circumstances of a state and the complex nature of implementation, can be strictly derived from the value lists cited. To do so would be to assume that all values are equal and noncontradictory.

Plans are not lists. They are patterns for orderly change. To be truly dynamic, they must embody a series of critical choices affecting the structure and content of the system that are responsive to overarching norms. Since all ends and needs are not equal or equally met, these choices must be among competing priorities and should be closely tied to political and fiscal exigencies. The plan when viewed in this light forms the impetus for change and bridges the gap between ideology and implementation.

What is suggested here is a plan that is substantively different from more conventional forms of planning. Characteristically, planning in the human service arena is focused on improved coordination, efficiency, and unification of services. Elimination of duplication and gaps in service delivery are by-words in this process. A good example of this form of planning is that being conducted by Health Services Agencies (HSAs) pursuant to PL 93-641. This planning procedure is aimed at controlling duplication of health facilities, coordinating existing health resources, and reducing the costs of unsystematic growth and utilization.

The plan envisioned for bringing about reform in the developmental disabilities field is qualitatively different. It is an instrument to guide the system through a transitional stage by describing how to get from here to there. It is plan for change. It should form the basis upon which administrators can navigate a course toward a new set of system activities whose content and assumptions are quite different from those that currently pertain. It is difficult to find examples of this type of planning. Perhaps efforts that come closest are those conducted by planners responding to court orders that mandate improvement in areas such as bilingual instruction, special education, and school desegregation. These plans are clearly aimed at changing the character of a system that is no longer acceptable and entail numerous transitional steps to reach the ultimate end of equal educational opportunity.

It is assumed that entry into this planning process is contingent on a finding by state officials that change is necessary in the system of care for developmentally disabled persons. The degree of change may vary, but the primary motivation for initiating planning in this context is to shift the focus of services from institutional care to a more balanced program in which large state-operated residential facilities are only one option in a multifaceted delivery system. This transition, of course, is made up of many steps—all interrelated and derived from the total plan design. The degree of change will depend on the current breadth, responsiveness, and sophistication of the state's efforts. States are now at differing levels of achievement, and the modifications necessary nationwide to create a more integrated service base range from moderate "tinkering" to significant alteration and redesign.

The plan, then, is a vehicle for justifying discrete critical choices that, once implemented, form the superstructure and content of the system that is to be. In the absence of these choices, the system grows and changes in an *ad hoc* fashion and is forced to survive in an environment dictated by earlier choices that may have little or nothing to do with the aims of reform. The areas where decisions are crucial include:

Organizing principle Planners must decide around what organizational construct the delivery of services will operate. Clearly, no system can be run from the top and bottom simultaneously. A choice must be made first about the degree of authority to be shared between the state and decentralized entities, and second, about what these decentralized entities will be. The first choice entails deciding the extent of discretion to be devolved and the second requires an identification of that local agency that is most likely, given particular state circumstances, to carry out the responsibility. Such agencies may include various sub-state organizations including local government, autonomous private agencies, state-run regional centers, or regional institutions.

Control In a transitional stage in particular, planners must decide who will exercise control and enforcement and in what ways. This choice is crucial to the stability of the balance of power between the state and a decentralized service system. Some states have opted to run services for developmentally disabled persons directly in order to maintain total control. Others have established regional state offices to oversee local governmental or private providers. Still others have established appointed citizen groups to monitor service delivery in various areas of the state.

Financial base Planners must review the fiscal methods for initiating, expanding, and maintaining services. A distinct choice here has a profound impact on the character of services provided and the capacity of the state to carry out resource development strategies. Several different methods have been explored in the states including grants-in-aid, capitation schemes, direct public provision, and reimbursement or fee-for-service.

Priorities Planners should also review the range for current and potential clients of the system. Choices then must be made among the competing needs of such client groups. The results may be a focus on institutional residents who can be prepared for community placements, or on persons living at home who are at risk of institutional placement, or a combination of the two. Priorities may also be fixed to degrees of disability or stages of intervention such as early identification, prevention, or amelioration. Since no state system can ultimately be all things to all people, this is a crucial albeit politically sensitive area of discretion.

Magnitude This is a decision that is very directly tied to an assessment of state resource limitations. It entails consideration of how significantly the system will change over time and the numbers of developmentally disabled persons that will be affected. Planners must determine how many persons can in fact be guaranteed appropriate community placements and for how many persons institutional care will remain a reality at least for the forseeable future.

Timetable Planners must describe the length of time that realistically will be entailed in the transition to a broader-based community system.

Clearly, some of these choices will have to be reexamined and perhaps altered as time goes on. The important thing is that they are made in proximity to one another and with an understanding of how one choice may affect the outcome of another. For instance, if seriously disabled persons are selected as a priority target group, then this has a direct impact on the length of time chosen to accomplish objectives and on the magnitude of change that can be carried out.

Two hypothetical state plans (Table 3-1) illustrate how these choices can be varied and the extent to which such choices are interrelated. In the case of State A, the choice was made to focus on the more seriously disabled institutional resident first—a choice that fits well with the structural aspects of a state-run system where continuity of responsibility is more direct and the problems of parent or family anxiety can be more easily assuaged. In State B, the locus of decision-making regarding priorities has

Table 3-1. Two hypothetical state plans

State A	State B
Organizing principle	
State-run system operating through regional multipurpose agencies	State and local government partnership with localities purchasing services from private providers
Control	
Uniform guidelines and criteria for service delivery, personnel recruitment, and other procedures; monitoring conducted by local citizen's organizations	General state guidelines setting overall procedures, service standards, and rates; local policies regarding service purchase, personnel, and system components; monitoring by state regional offices
Financing	
Direct line item appropriations to regional state agencies	Block grants to local governments based on local plans for service development; fee-for-service paid to providers by local government; start-up funds available to generate new services
Priorities	
Severely developmentally disabled persons currently residing in state institutions in the initial phase of the plan	Developmentally disabled young adults living in the community in need of training and alternative living arrangements in the initial phase of the plan
Magnitude	
Movement of 200 severely disabled institutional residents into twenty small state-run supervised group homes	Placement of 400 developmentally disabled young adults in vocational and training programs and the development of twenty group homes, fifty supervised apartment units, and ten ICF/MR facilities
Timetable	
Five years to accomplish the initial phase	Three years to accomplish the initial phase

been shifted to the local level where constituent pressure from parents of developmentally disabled persons residing in the community is more consistent with the priority set. Resource development in the former case is given a longer duration—a choice that is consonant with the target group selected and the bureaucratic complexities involved in initiating state-operated living arrangements. In the second case, the shorter time span is in keeping with the broader range of service providers available to localities, assuming, of course, that rates have been set at an equitable level and that funds have been appropriated in adequate amounts.

Failures in planning for system improvement to date can generally be explained by failures to make important critical decisions at the beginning of a reform effort and in some instances by an inadequate recognition of the force of choices that were made. Specific state examples include:

Nebraska Nebraska has been able to reduce its institutional population by about half since 1968. This was accomplished largely through the intensive efforts of the Eastern Nebraska Community Office of Retardation (ENCOR), one of six regional community-based mental retardation programs established under the Inter-Local Cooperative Act of 1963. However, neither the Act nor the Nebraska Citizen's Study Committee Plan, which led to the Act, delineated state control mechanisms, issues of magnitude, timetables, or priorities. Consequently, the regional programs and particularly ENCOR grew with little or no guidance. Each local unit has become a relatively autonomous entity overseeing its own service system largely under contract. There is little coordination among the regions and even less between the regions and the state.

California Though California now has a network of twenty-one regional centers for developmentally disabled persons, it is still constrained by a poorly defined system of state control and enforcement. In this case the choice of an organizing principle and a funding mechanism took precedence over other choices, leaving priority, magnitude, and timetable issues to be made on an *ad hoc* and unsystematic basis. The result is a relatively autonomous set of local organizations constantly in conflict with state policies and at odds with sporadic attempts at overall state administration.

Connecticut Perhaps more than most states in the country, Connecticut did construct a plan that by and large forced critical system decisions. It opted for state-run regional centers to organize local services; it reserved program control to the state by choosing to provide services by public employees; it established basic priorities; and it spelled out the magnitude of change over time. State administrators maintained the integrity of these choices and built policies and guidelines based on early choices. The only critique in this case is that state planners and decision-makers have not continued to inspect these original choices as time has gone by with the same vigor as the original planners. As a result there is a danger that the original dynamism may be dampened before the transitional phase has been completed.[1]

The design of a plan for system reform can take place in a variety of institutional settings that in turn slightly alter the content of the ultimate product. At the state level, planning may take place in the state legislature as well as in the executive branch—in the latter case in either a broad-based human service agency or in a categorical agency with sole responsibility for services to developmentally disabled persons. Planning can and does take place in state and federal courts as a result of litigation aimed at the rights of mentally disabled persons. At a local or regional level, planning may also be carried out by local government, citizen boards, or other designated entities. Each of these planning bodies has a different constituency and a different set of norms by which they operate. Such special circumstances must also be weighed by planners who are attempting to assess their role in overall system reform.

In sum, then, a plan is a constellation of choices that make up the pattern or design for system improvement. Making these choices, however, still is not sufficient to guarantee a systematic approach. Other concrete factors must also be assessed, and some of these key elements are discussed in the remainder of the chapter.

GOAL DEVELOPMENT

As just discussed, the plan for system improvement cannot be deduced merely from espoused values, but rather it is a separate entity responsive to internal state circumstances. The values stand outside the plan and, viewed as a whole, can be used to critique the integrity of the components of the plan. In this judgmental sense, the values or policies can be translated into ends that characterize the broad vision or ultimate aims of the plan. For instance, the policy of "equal justice" can be separated into the following ends:[2]

Full legal and civil rights for the developmentally disabled
Equal access to publicly supported generic services
Elimination of discrimination against qualified developmentally disabled persons who are seeking gainful employment

Goals within the plan are specific statements of expected results over time. They are not restatements of abstract ends. They form a constellation of interrelated objectives that should, when achieved, move the system as a whole toward ultimate aims. Thus, the ends of equal justice may be furthered by the accomplishment of several goals within the plan. Concrete objectives might include passage within two years of a bill of rights for developmentally disabled persons or the creation of specific fiscal incentives to attract generic agencies to the provision of services to this client group. These goals of course serve other ends including those associated with normalization and human dignity.

Keeping the dynamics between the internal goals and the external ends that stand apart from the plan is crucial to the systematic nature of the process. If planners continue to think broadly about these interrelated ends, then the goals in turn should fit into an equally well knit pattern. If this is the case, it is impossible to imagine a plan that has as a goal, movement of residents out of institutions without concomitant goals for resource development and client management. Moving persons out of institutions as a singular act is neither an end in itself nor is it a goal that can stand alone. It is only one possible step in the range of objectives necessary to achieve system reform and the ultimate integration of developmentally disabled persons into society.

How to treat deinstitutionalization is an issue for almost every state planner across the country. Most plans do or will contain some movement of persons from large facilities into smaller units in the community. In its most basic sense, deinstitutionalization means removing persons from institutional programs and placing them elsewhere. The connotation of the term has also been stretched to include the prevention of admission to large, more custodial residences. In both cases, however, the basic process is only one of many related activities that may be necessary to ensure the well-being of developmentally disabled persons in more normal settings.

By itself, deinstitutionalization is neither a value nor an end. It is neutral. It is a series of steps that once taken may or may not be beneficial to clients. The extent to which deinstitutionalization proves beneficial is solely contingent on the other objectives in the plan and the ways in which the total complex of goals assist in moving the existing system from here to there.

In the two hypothetical plans described in Table 3-1, it was possible to posit phases in the plan, at least in State B, that did not include deinstitutionalization *per se,* but that were attentive to the prevention of institutionalization. In the case of State A, deinstitutionalization was included but was proposed to take place as community living arrangements were made available. These plans represent only two ways of either reducing the negative effects of traditional institutional care or obviating the need for admission to such facilities. Specific goals in keeping with this intent might include closing admissions to institutions, dividing institutional programs into smaller units, or transferring residents to less restrictive and smaller state facilities. Again, these goal's cannot stand alone but must be coupled with other objectives. These additional goals might include the assignment of case management responsibilities to an accountable agency in the community, the development of quality assurance standards for community residences, and the allocation of funds sufficient to cover the start-up costs for residential programs.

Deinstitutionalization derives a positive value only when it is encompassed in a comprehensive set of goals that speak to general system values. In this context, the process can be viewed variously. Deinstitutionalization may be set as a goal for persons residing in large nursing care or domiciliary facilities. Here, it takes on a more generic connotation and is directed at institutions as such, whether run under state or private auspices. Conversely, a goal that is merely aimed at the movement of persons from a state institution to a private institution of similar size—assuming that smaller arrangements would be more appropriate—both violates the generic meaning of the term and is not responsive to overall ends.

Putting the deinstitutionalization process in this perspective reinforces the overall theme of this book—the plan for system improvement is a complex instrument that must be broadly viewed as a comprehensive design. Maintaining a vision of the values as ultimate ends of the planning process makes any singular goal that results in "dumping" automatically suspect. In the past, the failure to put deinstitutionalization in a systematic framework among equally important goals for reform has in fact resulted in only partial and, in some instances, detrimental change.

To reiterate, goals are statements that articulate the substance and direction of the critical choices discussed earlier. As such they should be quantifiable and time-limited in order to be subjected to ongoing monitoring. An important prerequisite to the development of goals is a sufficient base of information from which to make population and other quantifiable projections. Unfortunately, most state developmental disabilities authorities have not had access to such information and, therefore, have been reluctant to formulate precise goals. Lacking data, goals cannot be stated quantitatively, nor can their subsequent achievement be measured. As a consequence, too many plans have been based on vague statements of purpose or intent rather than precise objectives.

Goals should also be assigned priorities and linked to specific local, state, and federal funding streams. This step is essential in order to concentrate limited resources on the most important system improvement goals.[3] For example, the state of Washington has given priority to the reduction of inappropriate institutional admissions prior to the decrease of the institutional population. The state of Connecticut has acted first to shift mildly and moderately retarded persons to community residences. Pennsylvania and other states have given priority to the establishment of a community residential network as a basis for reductions in the institutional population and as a means for providing institutional alternatives for persons living in the community.

Once goals have been adopted and their effect projected, it is important to identify the principal constraints that are likely to hamper their realization. These constraints may include:

Economic constraints Obstacles to the availability or utilization of various funding streams

Legal constraints Pre-existing statutory or court orders that bind delivery system procedures

Political constraints Particular special interest constellations that may delay or distort system change (e.g., the interests of employee organizations)

The fact that goal development is treated early in this chapter is somewhat misleading. In one sense this presentation is backward, since goal development should in fact take place as a base of information becomes available through needs assessment and resource identification activities described subsequently. It is dealt with here because the goal-setting process is so crucial to the orientation of the plan. By describing goals within the larger context of values and ends, the pre-eminence of goal development is emphasized. In too many instances, this critical task is dictated solely by the availability of resources rather than by the ends of reform. In the framework proposed, the premises of goal development should determine all other planning activities even though the formulation of the precise wording of goals may occur once certain other planning activities are well under way.

NEEDS ASSESSMENT

Goal development and the planning process generally are dependent on information regarding the needs and characteristics of the population for whom services are to be provided. The conduct of a needs assessment has always been seen as the *sine qua non* of any planning activity. However, in this form of transitional or change-oriented planning it seems to have had only limited utility. The major critiques of needs assessments to date are: (1) many analyses are based on abstract national epidemiological statistics with a questionable relevance to particular state circumstances; (2) some needs assessment schemes are unfocused and result in the collection of odds and ends of information with no cohesion; and (3) almost all needs assessment projects include no differentiation between those whose needs are immediate and those needs are merely speculative.

Several factors have contributed to this result:

Needs assessments based on abstract statistics make no distinctions between individuals receiving services and those who are not

Most epidemiological statistics are based on federal government or national interest group data and are only sporadically updated to reflect changes in birth rates and changes in infant morbidity indicators

Most needs assessments are not sufficiently precise to allow planners to link incidence figures with particular service needs

In many instances needs assessments are conducted outside the developmental disabilities authority by such entities as the Developmental Disabilities Council and therefore do not necessarily become an integral part of planning for implementation

Some needs assessments can be derived from existing data sets in various state agencies, but this process is constrained by duplicated case counts, differences in labeling, and other inconsistent categorizations

Current survey techniques do not provide planners with data regarding potential demand among developmentally disabled persons and their families

To conduct a comprehensive needs assessment that provides unduplicated figures, includes information on level of disability, stipulates level of service received, and can be updated over time is an extremely costly undertaking

The fallacy of more abstract needs assessments in this area is that they presume a goal of universal coverage over time and the ability of the assessing entity to meet the needs that are uncovered. In the case of developmental disabilities authorities, these are clearly not operational assumptions. The expectation of universal coverage over time may in fact be an end or ultimate aim of planning generally, but it must stand outside the concrete plan. Planners must recognize that they have access to only limited resources and must select among competing needs. They must also be aware that they can only manipulate certain resources under their jurisdiction and should address themselves to those needs for which they can generate services—either directly or through interagency agreements.

The dilemma of attempting to use broad incidence data to discern specific service needs is characterized by this quote from the Connecticut Developmental Disabilities Plan:[4]

> At this time, Connecticut is unable to estimate how many developmentally disabled persons are not in service since sufficient

data has not been completed on how many persons are receiving services. Even with the latter information, it would be incorrect and unfair to assume that all other persons who are not presently receiving the services are in need of them. An example of this illogic is apparent in the situation of residential services. At this time 3,803 mentally retarded persons are receiving domiciliary care, and 849 are in special living arrangements. This total of 4,652 subtracted from the estimated total number of retarded persons, 47,049 leaves 42,397 that are *not* receiving residential services.

One explanation for the failure of abstract and fragmented needs assessment activities to inform and support the planning process in this field lies in the nature of the process itself. As discussed in the first part of this chapter, the plan is a design for change and reform, not just for service expansion and improved coordination. When looked at this way, the requirements for needs assessment are also altered. Planning for reform is not a matter of broadening the availability of existing discrete services. Rather, it entails a re-examination of the appropriateness of services currently being provided and a determination of what services in their place will more adequately meet the needs of developmentally disabled persons.

A good example of the use of needs assessment in this way as a prerequisite to design of system reforms can be seen in California's planning process in the mid-1960s. Prior to the initiation of legislation, the California Assembly Interim Committee on Ways and Means, Subcommittee on Mental Health Services conducted extensive surveys in state hospitals serving the mentally retarded and in the 225 private facilities serving this group. The surveys were comprehensive and elicited information about the facilities and the needs of clients receiving services. Public hearings were also held and parents of 1,200 children on state hospital waiting lists completed questionnaires for the Subcommittee.

In addition to those groups currently receiving services, it is also possible to identify particular at-risk populations where the probability of future or current service demand may be high. These groups might include disabled infants identified at birth through newborn high-risk registeries, developmentally disabled young adults graduating from special education programs, and adult developmentally disabled persons with aging or infirm parents. In any state system where resources are scarce, those persons whose needs are inevitable rather than hypothetical should be the focus of the assessment.

There are several avenues available to planners for data in the conduct of needs assessments to meet requirements in this area. One which has emerged through the passage of PL 94-142 (Education for All Handicapped Children Act) is the mandatory "Child Find" project in each state. This effort is intended to search out any disabled children in the state who are not enrolled in a special education program or whose current level of instruction is not appropriate. In addition to this initial effort, many states are also developing fairly sophisticated information systems to record individual educational plans (also mandated by the Act) and to monitor changes in the student's progress over time. For example, the Connecticut Department of Education is proposing to install a data collection system that will include information on education and related needs, services required to meet needs, agencies designated to provide services, time alloted for goal attainment, amount of service received by program, and appropriateness of placement. When this system is in operation, it will provide a rich source for evaluating service needs.[5]

Other sources of needs data may include local social service workers, protective service agencies, newborn registeries, and the individualized program plans now prepared by many state and local developmental disabilities agencies.

One area where focused needs assessment is important is in the political arena and specifically with state legislators. Merely presenting broad epidemiological data as a case for expanding services is both confusing and frustrating to decision-makers. This approach is likely to result in an attitude characterized by a "where will it all end" reaction. By presenting legislators with solid facts on populations most in need and most likely to benefit from services, the reform effort then can be portrayed as a more manageable and focused endeavor.

Finally, the planner who is canvassing potential service need must also be aware as time goes by that need can be created by particular policy or regulatory changes. For instance, the Developmental Disability Authority in California has raised rates for service providers. The new rates are higher than those currently paid by county social service agencies for certain types of home care. It is assumed that many of the county providers serving developmentally disabled persons will request that they now become vendors to the regional centers in order to increase their rates. This in turn will swell caseloads with newly identified developmentally disabled persons. Because the magnitude of the population in county-funded homes is unknown, it is almost impossible to anticipate new resource needs attendant on this change. This example illustrates the necessity of identifying numbers of developmentally disabled persons being served under other auspices in order to respond to such unexpected contingencies.

The actual content of the needs assessment is of course contingent on the scope of the plan and on particular state circumstances. There are, however, some basic ingredients that might be useful to think about:

A review of the current institutionalized population in state facilities to ascertain level of functioning, income levels, age, and potential for movement into less restrictive programs
A survey of developmentally disabled persons residing in private large institutional facilities to determine the appropriateness of ongoing placement and probable alternatives
A review of persons on waiting lists for public and private facilities to determine the characteristics of such persons and the possibility of alternatives to the service applied for
A survey of members of the state's developmental disabilities consumer groups to ascertain general needs as perceived by members and the specific needs of disabled children of members
Interviews with social and protective service workers to determine needs that they perceive among low income families with developmentally disabled children
A review of the results of " Child Find" activities to ascertain patterns of unserved children in various parts of the state
A survey of private proprietary and nonprofit agencies serving developmentally disabled persons to determine the provider assessment of need
A canvass of other data sources including high risk registeries, school records, offices on the aging, and vocational rehabilitation facilites

By regarding needs assessment as an integral part of the goal development activity, the form and content of the assessment should become much clearer. The goals, given the nature of the planning process described, are necessarily objectives that span a transitional period; they are dynamic and attentive to overall system ends. The needs addressed by the plan should therefore be tied to those groups whose circumstances are to be changed or whose life situation will at some point in the future propel them into a potentially inappropriate setting.

RESOURCE IDENTIFICATION AND DEVELOPMENT

Though clearly the availability of resources constrains the numbers of developmentally disabled persons that can be served and the range of needs that can be met, the limitations should not totally govern the conduct of goal development and needs assessment described earlier. By making resource identification preeminent, planners run the risk of perpetuating the status quo and overlooking previously unexplored avenues of support. This is not to say that the plan should raise expectations beyond practical realities. It is to say that the very nature of the transition envisioned by the enterprise requires the pursuit of a much broader array of resources than were at hand or even conceived of in a more narrowly defined system.

There are three major planning phases in the resource identification and development process:

Design of a comprehensive service network to meet needs and priorities
Exploration of sources of funds and resources
Assessment of probable costs and financing strategies

The service design phase is perhaps most clearly tied to the context of values and policies described earlier. Though they cannot alone determine the shape and content of any system, they can guide its broad outlines. Major concerns that flow from the adoption of these policies include the relative size of programs, the extent of their integration into regular community life, their ability to maximize individual potential, their age and cultural appropriateness, and their capacity to meet a multiplicity of social, habilitative, educational, and medical needs.

The program design is a crucial element in the overall plan because it defines the nature of the proposed transition in services. It is relatively easy to portray what has gone before, but articulating what will come after is much more challenging. This is doubly true when one realizes the staying power of such decisions in large bureaucracies. It requires a long view of developments in the field and an ability to differentiate between those trends that are merely passing fads and those with real staying power.

In addition to state-of-the-art considerations, there are also significant variables within states that must be taken into account in system design. Some of these concerns include:

Functional levels of clients to be served Each plan will presumably be directed at specific groups of clients with particular levels of disability, ages, and life experiences. These characteristics in turn dictate in large part the orientation and mixture of services to be delivered. If, for instance, a priority is placed on older more disabled persons coming out of institutions then the design should at least provide for supervised living arrangements, workshop programs, case management, resocialization services, and income support. On the other hand, if the focus is on early intervention, amelioration of disability, and prevention of institutionalization in young children, then the design components might include developmental day care, family resource services, infant stimulation services, genetic counseling, and intensive newborn nurseries.

Socioeconomic factors The culture and traditions of the state are important considerations in service design. Such things as the degree of urbanization, family stability, and levels of income are all factors that may affect the success of the design proposed. For instance, in some urban areas, the degree of family disorganization may prevent the maintenance or return of a significant number of developmentally disabled persons to their own homes. However, in more rural areas the family may be a valuable resource. In a recent study conducted in Alabama, 228 patients released from Bryce Hospital as a result of the *Wyatt v. Stickney* decision were followed up and monitored. Of all those sent back to the community, a full 72 percent returned to their own home where at least one family member resided. Very few of these ex-patients were readmitted.[6] Though these former residents were predominately mentally ill and not developmentally disabled, the results do point out that families should be taken seriously by many state planners as a significant resource to be strengthened and supported.

Level of saturation As part of the system design, planners must also be alert to the impact that various service locations will have on clients and the surrounding community. The problem of "ghettoization" of residential facilities for various disability groups has been well documented and should clearly be avoided. This requires a serious analysis of existing and proposed sites and a well developed strategy to scatter sites where necessary. In the past, resources have been developed in areas where resistance was lowest and where facility costs were minimal. Though this may be expedient in some cases, it should be tempered by a much broader strategy for overall service distribution.

Zoning and code restraints The problems of local zoning barriers and the multiplicity of building restrictions are also well known to officials who have attempted to develop residential resources. In some states, legislatures have passed statutes preempting local zoning ordinances. California's statute prohibiting discrimination against group, foster, and family care homes serving six or fewer persons is a case in point. By removing this major obstacle, the process of design is simplified. However, in some states such legislation is not politically feasible and the design must be developed to account for this hurdle. In many states, planners are now moving to the sheltered apartment concept in order to avoid both building code and zoning limitations. Other states, such as Connecticut, have chosen to operate group homes under state auspices, thus taking advantage of a state statute that exempts state facilities from local zoning.

Degree of cooperation with other agencies Since developmentally disabled persons require services from an array of providers once they are living in the community, planners must take into account the roles of other state and local entities in the overall design. If in fact other public and private providers are plentiful and cooperative, then the range of services to be provided by the developmental disabilities authority may be restricted to highly specialized programs. However, in areas where services are underfunded or nonexistent, the DDA may have to cajole other agencies into filling the gaps or, in the extreme, provide the missing support services first hand. The New Jersey Department of Institutions and Agencies recently avoided the latter dilemma in the area of rental support payments. Realizing that they did not have sufficient funds to pay for the maintenance of clients in a range of community living arrangements, staff from the agency approached the Department of Community Affairs in the hope of securing earmarked rental subsidy monies under Section 8 of the Housing and Urban Development Act. Community Affairs was responsive to the idea, and with the help of a Developmental Disabilities grant from the state Council they are now distributing funds to the mentally disabled. The success of this strategy greatly enhanced the scope of the current and future system design in the state.

Regardless of the individual state variables, however, it is important that the system design be governed by some unifying principles. Georgia's "communitization" plan, for instance, is premised on the movement of no more than four persons into small living arrangements, a heavy emphasis on family support, and individualized programming for every client.[7] Pennsylvania's design for resource development includes several priorities all built into a continuum of residential and support services. The entire system is premised on the principles of social and physical integration, diversification, separation of domiciliary and support service functions, and creation of social systems for developmentally disabled persons. The continuum of residential care includes home support, adoptive families, developmental maximization units, intensive habit-shaping homes, structured correctional homes, child development homes, long-term sheltered living, adult short-term homes, adult minimal supervision homes, and, finally, community living.[8]

Without a guiding orientation as a backdrop to system design, there is no coherence or integrity to the resource development process.

The second phase, exploration of sources of funding and resources, is discussed in part in the previous chapter, at least as regards federal funding. In addition to a careful canvassing of available federal monies, state planners should also survey other untraditional resources at the state level such as departments of community affairs, housing and finance, and employment. Those agencies do not necessarily count institutionalized persons among their constituencies. However, once developmentally disabled persons reside in the community, they should legitimately fall within the purview of these generic entities. The same holds true for a host of generic resources in the community including churches, schools, social clubs, senior citizen's centers, and public and private day care centers.

An analysis of existing manpower resources is another part of the planning process. It is important to identify new roles for existing personnel as well as to identify new sources of staff. Major roadblocks to successful change may develop if there is a failure to build mechanisms into the plan for smooth transitions of staff from more traditional functions to new roles in alternative services.

Pennsylvania, for example, has been unable to establish permanent or even *ad hoc* arrangements to permit the discharge of state institutional employees or their transfer to the county-administered programs in the local communities. This has contributed to disproportionately high institutional staff ratios in many of the institutions and a waste of funds that could be more productively redeployed in local communities. The effective denial of these staff resources to the community programs has severely constrained the development of the community care network.[9]

The final phase of this planning component entails the assessment of costs for proposed resources. A recent report by the Environmental Design Group in Boston presents a good example of cost analysis based on state resource needs. This document, which was prepared for the Massachusetts Office of Mental Retardation, outlines not just one strategy but several for solving the problems presented by an institutional system substantially out of compliance with federal life-safety standards. It offers state planners a series of options from total institutional compliance to varying levels of deinstitutionalization of current residents. Each option describes costs and the relative numbers of developmentally disabled persons affected.[10]

An assessment of costs should also include those start-up funds necessary for new or expanded services. Before any program can open its doors, it must be planned, organized, and staffed; equipment and facilities must be obtained; and operating procedures must be established. Even after the program begins operations, there will be a period of testing and growth prior to realizing its planned potential. In the absence of some start-up funding, the field of potential community-based providers is narrowed to those with other sources of capital or large agencies that rely on savings from other enterprises to cover new construction and service development. In any case, the new provider will eventually have to find some way of recovering start-up costs or suffer the financial consequences of failing to do so. Possible solutions to the problem of start-up costs that state officials may wish to consider during the planning phase include:

Establishment of state mortgage guarantees for a portion of new facility costs

Issuance of state construction bonds with the proceeds to be allocated according to some kind of lease-purchase plan (although the competition for this money is usually high and the amount limited)

Provision of low-cost financing directly to private sponsors for the construction or renovation of community residential facilities

Development of state-run services with start-up funds allocated directly from the state legislature[11]

A state also might assist potential providers in seeking private capital by guaranteeing the providers in writing that a specified number of clients will be referred to them at acceptable reimbursement rates. Methods of prospective reimbursement may also be explored to offer providers some collateral for purposes of securing long-term financing. Again, however, some provision must be made to reimburse the providers for legitimate start-up costs, or their financial problems will simply be postponed.

The Canadian National Institute on Mental Retardation, with the sponsorship of the Canadian Association for the Mentally Retarded, has developed a deinstitutionalization plan, entitled *A Plan for Comprehensive Community Services (COMSERV) for the Developmentally Handicapped*, that provides demonstration grants to support start-up costs. The plan includes a specific set of guidelines for comprehensive plans and budget requests from community and regional sponsors for the purpose of developing community services as alternatives to institutionalization. Comprehensive community service proposals consistent with the guidelines and identified community needs may be approved as demonstration projects for subsequent evaluation. If the programs are successful, continuing support is provided through other channels.

Financial resources may be allocated to planned programs in a variety of ways, of which two are:

Categorical or block grant funding Funds may be allocated as grants to support a program of services based on plans generated by the counties or other local entities responsible for the generation of resources at the local level. This is the method currently employed in Pennsylvania's mental health and mental retardation system. Its advantage is that essential start-up costs may be provided as part of the program grant. On the other hand, it tends to weaken the state's ability to control the level of services to be provided individual clients.

Purchase-of-service Under this arrangement, operating agencies are reimbursed according to the level of services provided or to be provided (prospective reimbursement) in line with an established fee schedule. The schedule should be structured to induce the providers to serve the developmentally disabled on the same basis as other disabled or disadvantaged clients and should adequately cover all provider costs. Because this is so important to the success of the purchase-of-service approach, the plan should encourage regular review and adjustment of reimbursement rates. Failure to build in such flexibility could lead to the problems now facing the developmental disabilities authority in California as it struggles with a new legislative mandate to develop a more responsive rate schedule. The Legislature became concerned after numerous complaints from providers suggested that rates had neither kept pace with actual costs nor with rates being offered by other agencies administering purchase-of-service contracts.[12] Too often, reimbursement rates are held down as a means of controlling program costs when other, more effective methods have not been developed.

Problems entailed in securing additional state appropriations and the political issues involved are discussed in subsequent sections.

ENDORSEMENTS AND NEGOTIATION

The plan for system improvement should have at least the tacit endorsement and preferably the explicit support of those key individuals and organizations whose cooperation is necessary for implementation. A politically feasible plan must take into consideration:

The costs and the benefits of all proposed changes for clients, providers, administrators, communities, and employees

The relative acceptability of particular policy changes to each of the above groups
The power that each of the groups can wield to inhibit or assist implementation of the plan

This type of analysis will help planners to see the incentives and benefits that can be used to persuade various groups of the virtues of the plan. Incentives to providers may include technical assistance, a guarantee of stable or increased fee schedules, guaranteed program funding, control over institutional admissions, or expanded staff. Incentives to consumer groups may include a client advocacy system, new or expanded services, an improved client management system, and expanded community services. Incentives to program administrators may include development of an improved information system, installation of an advanced management system, and increases in service efficiency.

Incentives to the local communities affected by the proposed changes may include a reduction in the local tax burden and an increase in local control over service decisions. Institutional employees may be drawn to the plan because it includes retraining programs, improved working conditions, job placement services, job guarantees, pension protection, portability of benefits, early retirement, and/or advancement opportunities.

In order to secure the endorsement of elected officials the plan must not only be acceptable to their constituents but it also must address itself directly to fiscal concerns. Where reliable information is available, it may be presented as a vehicle for long-range savings. At least is should reflect an attempt to make maximum use of all available resources. It should also include accounting procedures that will produce a clear picture of how state and other funds are being spent, for whom, and for what services. As the community-based program for developmentally disabled persons grows, legislators will increasingly demand accounting of where dollars are going and to what end.

Other factors may influence public officials to support and endorse the goals of the plan. In a number of states, key elected officials who actively work for improvement of the system have been influenced by personal experiences with developmentally disabled persons. In some states, such as Nebraska, Georgia, and Connecticut, associations for retarded citizens have mounted public awareness campaigns to gain support for changes in the delivery system among elected officials and the general public. In other states, officials have been persuaded of the merits of a proposed change after being exposed to the conditions in state institutions. It should be realized, however, that such exposure may have the opposite effect; elected officials may concentrate solely on upgrading conditions in the state schools and hospitals and defer action on community-based programs.

The commitment of elected officials and high-level state administrators is crucial to a plan's acceptance by staff in the state's bureaucracy who will be responsible for carrying it out. Many state employees have seen sweeping reform activities fail and are therefore somewhat cynical about the possibility of real change. This cynicism can lead them to give no more than token cooperation in critical areas of implementation.

Elected officials may be reluctant to publicly endorse significant changes if they clearly run counter to the expressed wishes of powerful interests. For instance, the announced closing of state hospitals in California and Pennsylvania in recent years generated substantial outcries from employee and other organizations. This opposition could have been anticipated, however, and state planners should have been prepared to give legislators details about the costs and benefits of the proposed changes, ways in which the well-being of the clients was to be protected, and other information necessary to counter opposition to reform.

Where state officials have been hesitant to endorse proposed reforms, there has been a tendency to adopt plans that require a relatively limited investment or that can be carried out on a trial or pilot basis. In this way, if the changes prove successful within a limited area, they can be expanded later to other segments of the system at considerably less risk. If they are not successful, the costs and disruption of the existing system will have been minimized.

In California, changes in the system began with the establishment of two pilot regional centers for a limited trial period. The centers provided client diagnostic services, family counseling, client supervision and management, and other services purchased on behalf of clients. When it proved to be successful, the model was expanded statewide. Although the demonstration strategy worked in this case, it should be noted that it was begun almost thirteen years ago. Today, the impetus for change is stronger, and information on the efficacy of community-based programs is much more plentiful. These facts, coupled with the immediacy of other pressures for change such as the new ICF/MR standards, may mean that states no longer have the luxury to "wait and see."

The result of a failure to gain the endorsements of important decision-makers before a plan is implemented can be seen in the North Carolina experience.[13] The State's plan for deinstitutionalization centered on the creation of child advocacy centers to: (1) assist residential institutions to improve internal procedures, (2) reduce institutional populations, and (3) reduce inappropriate institutional admissions. Services to mentally retarded citizens in the State traditionally had been provided through the State's regional mental retardation centers. It was at these regional centers that the child advocacy program was installed. Each child advocacy center consisted of a director, three senior staff, and a small support staff. Plans for resident transfers were developed in collaboration with the staff of each regional mental retardation facility. Although specific approaches differed in each location, the basic design provided for the training of staff to prepare residents for community placement and to develop exemplary programs or projects to accomplish overall goals.

In practice, however, the advocacy programs were not successful in establishing durable procedures to increase community placements and decrease institutional admissions. Two of the three institutions totally rejected all training and program development activities. Only a handful of institutional residents were shifted to community programs as a direct result of the activities of the advocacy program, and the state's system is still predominantly one of large institutions. Within three years of its initiation, those opposed to the advocacy program had applied sufficient pressure to force its demise. The principal reason for the opponents' success was that the project lacked the support of state and local administrators who did not agree with its basic purpose. Additionally, even though some elected officials had given "lip service" to its goals, the project was not given adequate fiscal support. In the end, the advocacy centers, which were seen as threats to the continuing existence of the regional centers, proved to have no power base of their own and were ultimately abolished.

Though some improvements can be made in the delivery of services to developmentally disabled persons without the wholehearted support of key leaders, comprehensive change, short of litigation, is doomed to failure.

MONITORING

To ensure the efficient implementation of the various elements of the plan, it is necessary to build monitoring provisions into the planning process. Planners should develop methods for obtaining a continuing flow of information about progress toward full implementation of the plan so that they can quickly spot any deviations that might require refinement and modification. In order to do such "fine tuning," staff responsible for monitoring the implementation of the plan should be fully conversant in all of its aspects and the rationale behind each step. They must also be cognizant of the effect that delays or mistakes in one area may have on the successful accomplishment of the remaining goals in the plan. For instance, if there are problems in securing federal funds for a particular aspect of the system design, then resource development may be held up, the movement of clients out of institutions may be slowed, and other funding such as ICF/MR may be jeopardized. Unless all of these factors are taken into account, contingency planning is impossible.

In order to monitor progress, it is important to break each objective or goal into a series of tasks necessary for the accomplishment of a particular objective. In order to generate twenty group homes for 100 institutional clients, the following tasks may be entailed:

Assess appropriate locations for homes
Arrive at a design and standards for the homes
Explore relevant zoning and building code restrictions
Assess the relative cost advantages as between construction and utilization of existing facilities
Locate and train house parents for group homes
Develop a total plan for each individual resident that entails all available resources in the area
Develop rates of reimbursement
Assess probable cost trade-offs as among ICF/MR, SSI, and other funding sources
Work with parents and friends of developmentally disabled persons slated to reside in the homes
Develop transitional and predischarge planning procedures in the institution
Work with community leaders in the locales where homes will be established

Once tasks have been devised, then specific individuals should be made responsible for the accomplishment of each. In this way, those monitoring the plan can determine who is directly accountable for results. Too many plans have failed in the past because this accountability factor was missing. Spelling out specific expectations for everyone involved in the process also gives all actors a role and reinforces their identity and commitment to the whole.

In addition to task assignment, officials should set dates for the accomplishment of goals. Since it is assumed that the total plan will include a range of proposed activities and dates, it will be important to synchronize time lines to ensure that steps that facilitate or are prerequisite to other events are arranged in proper sequence.[14]

The creation of time schedules should also take into account the termination as well as the initiation of interim organizations and actions. For instance, if a blue ribbon committee is appointed to review compliance with evolving residents rights standards in the state's institutions, provision should also be made for its eventual replacement by a permanent advocacy mechanism.

Failure to differentiate between the short and long term may pose problems. A case in point is Pennsylvania, which established a statewide network of coordinators to expedite the development of community living arrangements for developmentally disabled persons. This network, which was a part of the state's design for deinstitutionalization, supplanted the county base service units that were legally responsible for case management functions. While the coordinators have proved quite effective in accomplishing their mission, it is unclear whether or not they are to continue to operate once a system of community residences has been developed and, if so, whether they will eventually be integrated into the county program. This uncertainty has caused conflicts between county and state administrators, especially as the role of the coordinators has expanded to include the development of support services in addition to residential arrangements.

Although state officials and administrators will want to stay in close touch with the planning process, it may be wise to designate another body to monitor the day-to-day operations. For example, in some states, the Developmental Disabilites Council may have sufficient expertise to perform this function. Inasmuch as these councils are representative of many different interests, they can ensure monitoring from a variety of vantage points. Moreover, their membership includes representatives from a variety of state agencies whose assistance may be required from time to time to facilitate funding or service coordination.[15]

This description of the various tasks involved in monitoring the plan as it is implemented reinforces the importance of a stable central office staff that understands and preferably lives through the initial planning activity. Since the transition described in the plan is likely to include many new and complex activities, the process of implementation is likely to be demanding. New staff or those unfamiliar with the antecedents of the plan will undoubtedly be at a disadvantage in guiding its practical application. Connecticut, which has enjoyed relative success in implementing a plan designed over a decade and a half ago, has enjoyed unusual staff longevity and relatively low turnover. Officials in the state feel that this positive factor has contributed heavily to their progress.[16]

EVALUATION

Monitoring, as described in the preceding section, is an internal management tool useful in marking task accomplishment and the relative progress toward specified goals. It is necessarily internal because it contributes to the day-to-day administration of plan activities. Evaluation, on the other hand, is essentially a process that is external to the day-to-day plan implementation activities. Evaluators are concerned with the effect that the implementation of the plan has had on the whole environment in which the plan is operating rather than on the timely and successful conduct of a particular task. It is up to an evaluator to investigate the extent to which outcomes of the plan are in fact consistent with the original ends of the process as a whole.

The ends of the planning process, as discussed in the initial section of this chapter, represent the overarching values and policies that form the context in which the planning process takes place. They do not dictate goals *per se*, but they can be used to evaluate or judge the character of these goals as they unfold in implementation. Just as ends can be derived from values, criteria can be derived from ends and used to measure relative progress. For example, the ends of equal justice might be assessed using the criteria[17] listed in Table 3-2.

Table 3-2. Assessing ends of equal justice

Ends	Criteria
Full legal and civil rights for the developmentally disabled	Are developmentally disabled persons represented by counsel in proceedings for involuntary commitment? Guardianship? Conservatorship? Abuse or mistreatment?
	Are developmentally disabled persons in treatment facilities informed of their rights?
	To the extent of their capabilities, are developmentally disabled persons given the right to make decisions affecting their lives? Vote? Marry? Manage their own funds?
	Do conservatorship and guardianship procedures adequately protect the rights of those developmentally disabled persons judged incompetent to manage their own affairs?
Equal access to publicly supported generic services	Are developmentally disabled persons granted access to public education programs on a nondiscriminatory basis?
	Are developmentally disabled persons granted equal access to generic human service programs such as social services, recreation, health maintenance, income maintenance, public residential programs, etc.?
Elimination of discrimination against otherwise qualified developmentally disabled persons in gainful employment	Do mechanisms exist for the recruitment and placement of developmentally disabled persons in gainful employment?
	Are employers held legally responsible if found guilty of discrimination against the developmentally disabled?
	Does a developmentally disabled person have access to the judicial process if he or she has been discriminated against?

In addition to an inspection of the general ends of the planning process, there are several other issues that may concern evaluators including:

Any political, funding, resource, or other constraint that has hampered the implementation of the plan
Measurable impact of particular activities on the levels of functioning and well-being of clients and their families
Particular legislative or regulatory changes that may be necessary to facilitate implementation
Recent or proposed changes in federal policy or case law that may affect implementation
The impact of plan activities on other areas of service delivery not directly included in the plan
The need for possible expansion, contraction, or revision of the current plan
The experience in other states where planners are operating under similar goals
The reaction of various consumer and other constituencies to the conduct of planning activities

There are several groups outside the developmental disabilities authority capable of addressing some or all of the evaluation components described. To the extent possible, such evaluators should be free from potential conflicts of interest growing out of any special relationship to the system. Clearly, no one is entirely free from conflicts or even ideological biases. As long as the evaluator prefaces an analysis with those affiliations or orientations likely to color the results, then it is up to the reader to assess their influence on any recommendations.

Some of the groups that may have the capability to conduct evaluations or to fund evaluation efforts include:

Developmental Disabilities Councils
Consumer organizations
Professional policy consultants
Public interest groups (including the League of Women Voters, law centers for the handicapped, etc.)
Professional organizations (National Association of Social Workers, the American Adademy of Pediatrics, etc.)
HEW regional offices through professional contracts
Universities
United Crusade

This is, of course, only a partial list but does show the range of organizations that can be brought to bear on the evaluation process.

One final form of evaluation that is conducted on an ongoing basis in many states is legislative monitoring. Though the legislature may in fact have created the broad outlines of the plan in the first place, it is not responsible for management or implementation. Legislators, therefore, are not in the same conflict position as are plan managers, who also assume the role of evaluators. Additionally, the legislature in most states is not a static body and therefore does not represent a unified and continuing posture on issues that might prevent a fresh analysis. The California legislature has perhaps been the most tenacious in monitoring the course of planned changes over time. Legislative studies of the implementation of legislative reforms designed in 1965 in that state were conducted in 1970 and 1976. Both of these assessments led to significant changes in law and regulation.

Regardless of the auspices under which evaluation is conducted, it is a key element in the planning process and should be fostered and supported whenever possible. Failure to be open to evaluation activities signals shortsightedness regarding the complexity of the task at hand and an inability to accept the inevitable difficulties involved in this transitional effort. It is too easy to become isolated in an activity of this magnitude and intensity. Fresh visions are necessary to keep the planning effort continually attentive to its original ends.

CONCLUSION

Carrying out a plan to bring about significant changes in the service system for developmentally disabled persons is a turbulent process demanding constant management attention. It is also a far-reaching process requiring the coordination of a myriad of providers, agencies, client advocates, case managers, and other participants. Finally, it is a process that calls for advanced management, communication, and technical skills to deal with the great range of tasks involved.

The next chapter describes the implementation process and its relationship to the plan. It also highlights four important elements in the process of system reform—management, resource development, quality assurance, and coordinated client management.

NOTES

1. See Lewin and Associates, Inc./Human Services Research Institute (Work-in-progress pursuant to Contract 72-76-HEW-0S), *Deinstitutionalization of Mentally Retarded and Other Developmentally Disabled Persons: An Assessment of Experience in Five States.*
2. For a proposed list of ends matched to each of the values suggested in Chapter II, see Appendix III.
3. John W. Ashbaugh, *Mental Health and Mental Retardation Program Planning Budgeting Procedure* (Washington, D.C.: Warburton-Ashbaugh Associates, 1976).
4. Connecticut, *State Plan for Developmental Disabilities and Facilities Construction Program for Fiscal Year 1977*, p. 24, Attachments, 2.2, 2.3.
5. Connecticut State Department of Education, *A State Plan for Special Education*, Volume I, Sections 1–11, Revised December 1, 1976, pp. 1–5.
6. Philip Leaf, Ph.D., "Patients Released After *Wyatt*: Where Did They Go?", *Hospital and Community Psychiatry*, Vol. 28, No. 5, May 1977, pp. 366–369.
7. Georgia, *Initial Guidelines for the Communitization Process* (DRAFT), May 1, 1977.
8. Mel Knowlton, Pennsylvania Office of Mental Retardation, *Developing a Statewide System of Community Living Arrangements*, Background paper for the NACSPMR Seminar, "Developing a Statewide System of Community Living Arrangements," November 4–7, 1977.
9. Mel Knowlton, *Community Living Arrangements and Policy Options*, Office Memorandum, May 20, 1977.
10. Environmental Design Group, *Campus Futures in the Balance: Massachusetts State Facilities for the Mentally Retarded*, prepared for the Massachusetts Department of Mental Health, 1976.
11. This tactic has been utilized in the states of Connecticut and Georgia.
12. California Legislature, Assembly Permanent Subcommittee on Mental Health and Developmental Disabilities, "Rates for Community Care Facilities for the Developmentally Disabled," March 1976.
13. This case example is excerpted from G. Ronald Neufeld, Ph.D., et al. (eds.), *Deinstitutionalization: Programs and Policy Development* (New York: Syracuse University Press, 1977).
14. A PERT (Program Evaluation and Revision Technique) chart may be helpful here. For an example see Office of Economic Opportunity Manual, *PERT for CAA*.
15. The Georgia Developmental Disabilities Council has adopted the monitoring role in recent months and will oversee a comprehensive evaluation of deinstitutionalization activities in that state.
16. Lewin and Associates, Inc./Human Services Research Institute, *op.cit.*
17. For a suggested list of policies, ends, and criteria, see Appendix III.

IMPLEMENTATION
Chapter four

Just as the plan must be a systematic document reflecting the multifaceted process of system reform, implementation activities must also be highly structured and cohesive. In fact, the line between designing the plan and implementing changes is very fine. Implementation entails continued planning and modification at increasingly specific levels of administration. Inherent in each step is replanning (i.e., rethinking) to ensure the ongoing relevance of application to the original ends of reform. As the actual tasks outlined in the plan are carried out, all must be coordinated and monitored to ensure the overall integrity of the enterprise envisioned.

Implementation, then, commences a transitional phase during which time significant changes will be brought about in the system of care for developmentally disabled persons. In addition to the specific changes proposed in the plan, other subtle and not so subtle changes can be anticipated as the implementation process takes place. Whenever a major shift of this magnitude occurs, it affects a whole constellation of pre-existing institutional and political relationships.

One important reorientation that has taken place in those states that have begun the reform process—and which can be anticipated in those states about to take the initial steps—is the change in relationships between the developmental disabilities authority and its traditional constituency. In most states, the DDA has operated in a closed system composed of the central office staff and institutional administrators. With an expansion and decentralization of services, these relationships are altered and DDA personnel are forced into an outward versus inward-looking posture. Within their own agency, staff must expand liaison activities beyond institutional programs and out to an array of agency-funded residential and support services. Outside of the agency, DDA personnel should be attentive to the major generic agencies in the state such as welfare, housing, and vocational rehabilitation to ensure that DDA clients are included in these programs.

Because of the infusion of new constituencies and the inherent change of focus embodied in the plan, polarizations in the system are likely to be exacerbated unless managers of the implementation process are successful in fully communicating their intentions and the rationale for actions to be taken. Some of the polarizations that may be affected include DDA vs. private providers, private providers vs. institutions, DDA vs. other state agencies, DDA vs. local government, and consumer groups vs. DDA. All of these conflicts emerge out of what are perceived as competitive roles in the new system rather than co-equal participation. If these conflicts become institutionalized, they may prove mortal to the accomplishment of goals and objectives.

Strains occur during the implementation process when the form and content of the plan have not been shared fully with potential participants. If the various constituencies sense that something is being held back, then they are likely to be fearful of what the ultimate implications are for their particular interests. A prime example of the problems created by this failure to divulge the basic plan outlines can be seen in the experience of Pennsylvania. Pennsylvania's Department of Public Welfare has recently moved to set up pilot areas to demonstrate the feasibility of institutional phase-downs and deinstitutionalization in the area of mental health. Though some progress has been made, the whole process was significantly crippled by years of uncertainty, mixed messages, and false starts coming from the central office. By the time the pilot began, the climate of distrust and suspicion had already been established, and groups such as the institutional employees continued to fight the pilot approach at every stage of its development.[1]

The new roles and responsibilities created through implementation may also force a reassessment of staff skills and functions within the central office. With the growth of a community-based service network, there will clearly be a need for state expertise beyond that required to manage an institutional system. Merely shifting personnel and titles will probably not be sufficient to ensure that the DDA is in a position to provide technical assistance to burgeoning community programs. There is also a more subtle issue here. If central office staff are to exercise control and guidance over new local services, such staff should command the respect of those persons working at the client level. Unless the "workers in the trenches" sense that state staff are knowledgable regarding delivery issues and problems, the legitimacy of central office direction may be questioned and the implementation process may be jeopardized.

In a state-run system, such as that in Connecticut, conflicts between the state and local or regional providers are obviously not as great since everyone is playing on the same team. Where this is not the case, the structural realities are likely to cause tension in even the best-run system. In California, the situation is compounded because there is an intervening layer between the state and local providers—the autonomous, nonprofit regional centers. The centers have been allowed to grow with little formal direction. Now that the state is moving to standardize service delivery, these reasonably independent bodies are extremely resistant.

Because many states have at least taken tentative steps in the direction of reform, it is possible to identify the major weaknesses in implementation activities to date:

A lack of thorough preparation of all constituencies regarding the orientation, substance, and rationale of the plan and, in some instances, a failure to convince participants of the seriousness of the endeavor

A failure on the part of the planners and officials to trust the integrity and validity of the enterprise in which they are involved, thereby leaving themselves vulnerable to shifting political winds and the force of opposing groups

A tendency to surrender the systematic direction of the plan to the day-to-day crisis management practiced in too many states

A lack of cohesion and coordination among key actors in the system

A failure to understand the necessity of replanning and modification as the system unfolds

All of these pitfalls reinforce the need for a systematic approach to the management of program reform and the importance of creating a variety of accountable and durable administrative structures that can withstand the pressures of this significant undertaking.

In order to ensure proper implementation of the plan described in the preceding chapter, four major system components must be designed: (1) implementation management units, (2) a resource development process, (3) a quality control component, and (4) a client management structure. Each of these components is critical to the eventual attainment of system reform goals because their presence in the system guarantees continuity of implementation, focused strategy for the generation of needed services, compliance with relevant quality of safety standards, and expeditious coordination of client needs for appropriate services.

The following four sections describe each of these system components in detail, including the major principles that should guide their design, the significant constraints that have hampered their implementation in the past, examples of the experiences of individual states, and suggestions in each case for new approaches to their design and implementation.

IMPLEMENTATION MANAGEMENT

Rarely is a traditionally organized state management system equipped to meet the demands of a truly comprehensive plan for the creation of a more balanced and humane service system. Designated teams of managers to supervise implementation of the plan are essential to bring about comprehensive change in an efficient and expeditious fashion (see Figure 4-1). To be most effective, these managers should be freed to the extent possible from line responsibility for the day-to-day administration of the system, although they must, of course, be knowledgable about the workings of the system.

Management units should be the focal point for all activities outlined in particular portions of the plan. This concentration of responsibility will encourage the integration of the various strategies being carried out and should result in more systematic activity. The implementation managers should be involved in all major decisions concerning costs, timing, plan refinement or modification, and the consummation of interdepartmental agreements. They should become involved at the very beginning of the planning process, and they should continue to oversee implementation through the critical two- to five-year transitional phase.

By establishing implementation management teams, state officials can be assured that someone is accountable for the accomplishment of each group of changes. This accountability should not be diluted by allowing these managers to be diverted to resolving rises in the ongoing operation of the system. Such "crisis management" has been characteristic of efforts to deinstitutionalize developmentally disabled persons, making those efforts extremely susceptible to external pressures of many kinds.

Pennsylvania's community-living coordinator network, which was mentioned earlier, provides a good example of an implementation management structure to oversee the accomplishment of the goals in the area of residential development. In April 1972, the Pennsylvania Office of Mental Retardation received an appropriation of $1.9 million for the establishment of community living arrangements (CLAs) as an alternative to institutional care. Since that time, the CLA budget has grown to $16.1 million and is projected to jump to $23 million in fiscal year 1977–1978. The

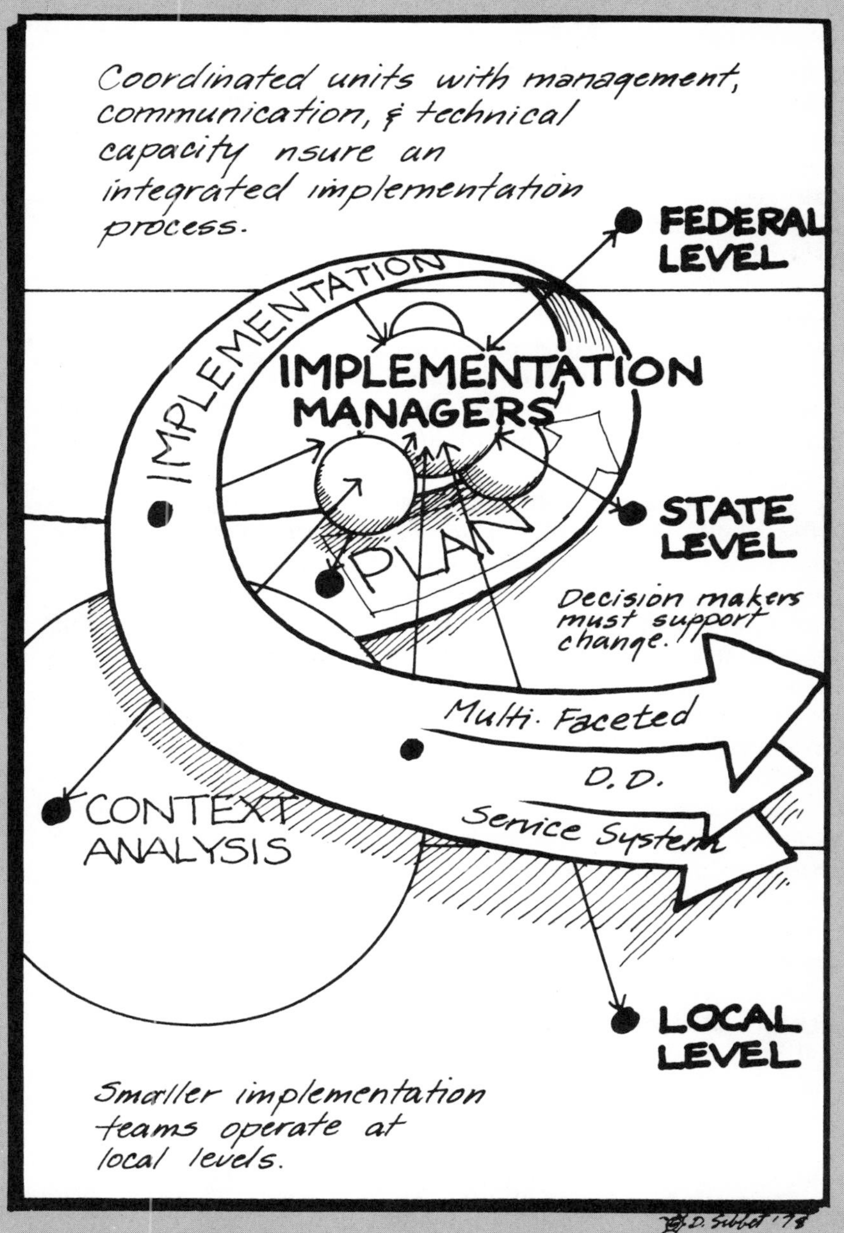

Figure 4-1. Process model.

program currently serves approximately 2,738 residents, 1,342 of whom were formerly institutionalized.[2] At the state level, one person has the sole responsibility for planning and implementing the development of community living arrangements throughout the state. A regional CLA coordinator is located in each of the four state regional offices, and forty-one CLA coordinators (CLACs) were established in each of the county administrative units. Unfortunately, the program suffers because of uncertainty about the permanence of the coordinators. Implementation managers, more because of the transitional nature of their tasks, may be more effective if they are regarded as serving in a temporary capacity.

The management team, in carrying out its responsibilities to achieve a particular objective, should prepare detailed working plans and budgets responsive to the requirements of specific goals. These working plans should indicate what is to be accomplished, by whom, when, and with what resources. By doing so, they will reflect the level of detail and precision required for actual implementation of the general plan and facilitate the division of labor among members of the management team. Given the comprehensive nature of the planned reforms, however, these working plans must be flexible enough to ensure that they remain responsive to the requirements of the general plan.

To protect the flexibility of the general plan, the managers should have latitude to reallocate a significant portion of state support from one objective or program to another as the need arises. Characteristically, the managers will be forced to work under severe time and budget pressures and will not have the opportunity in some instances to return to the legislature to secure revised budget directions. Granting managers this power is of course contingent on legislative approval and the endorsement of key legislators of the general goals in the plan. This latitude has been granted in limited areas. In Connecticut, for instance, administration of the state's multipurpose regional centers have the ability to move funds from one program area to another through the course of the year as needs dictate.

In the case of the community living program in Pennsylvania, implementation plans are updated annually based on state policy and budget guidelines and on information contained in county plans. The county plans are developed by the state CLACs and reflect local residential needs and funding priorities as well as specific state objectives and priorities. The coordinators, who are, in effect, implementation managers, ensure that the requisite number of institutional residents are placed in newly developed services and that CLA funds are spent for delegated purposes.

Through the monitoring system, managers should be alerted to deviations from implementation plans in time to take remedial action. Such feedback can be obtained through personal contacts, written reports, and meetings. At the same time, the managers must keep higher level decision-makers abreast of significant accomplishments and problems that may call for action. This is generally accomplished through the submission of periodic formal reports. The regular reports may be augmented by special reports or communications as needed to initiate urgent remedial actions or to respond to special decision-maker information requests.

Finally, the implementation managers also have an important role in securing the cooperation of other local, state, and federal agencies that have an interest in the implementation of the plan. In most states, managers will not have the authority to directly control most of these agencies; their role is largely one of mediation rather than direction. In some instances, where the manager is given more authority, he or she may be able to mandate cooperation among legally subordinate organizations. In the role of mediator, however, the manager must rely heavily on personal influence or political and fiscal inducements to develop productive linkages among individual organizations. The influence of the manager can be greatly enhanced if interagency agreements are secured in the initial planning phases. When this has been accomplished, managers can devote their efforts to monitoring compliance with such agreements and proposing revisions as necessary.

RESOURCE DEVELOPMENT

An important ingredient missing from the process of system reform in many states has been a concerted and centralized resource development effort within the DDA. Too many states have assumed that the availability of funds would be sufficient to generate the necessary resources—that is, the many services required by developmentally disabled persons. They have been right only in part; services have been developed but frequently not in sufficient quantity nor in all areas of need. By allowing the marketplace to determine the supply of services, these states have abdicated their responsibility to ensure an adequate supply of appropriate services of high quality.

Resource development is, of course, predicated on a systematic conception of a total service network and its specific needs and priorities.[3] Therefore, the development of this component must follow completion of the planning process described in the previous section. Resource development entails not only the development of new resources but also an expanded and more productive use of existing resources. Those states that have been most successful at developing their service resources have been those that have:

Fully utilized all existing sources of funding, including local, state, federal, and other third-party aid, to generate and support services

Systematically reduced institutional populations, thereby freeing state funds for the expansion of community services

Significantly increased the state's financial investment in the program

Actively encouraged interagency agreements to maximize the use of generic services

Substantially increased the availability of less costly community alternatives including those most likely to maintain developmentally disabled persons in their own homes

Use All Available Funds

There is a funding reservoir available to most states, derived from federal and other third-party sources, that amounts to a significant potential supplement to existing state and local financial resources. A careful analysis of these sources, as described in Chapter 2, can assist state officials in capturing significant augmentations to state and local funding. Securing these funds, however, should not be seen as a means of relieving a state's fiscal burdens but as a way of facilitating the accomplishment of system improvement goals. In other words, strategies for securing federal funds should entail more than simply maximizing dollars for the development of a community-based system. State officials should also explore ways of using federal funds to deal with some of the nonfinancial difficulties encountered in developing such a system.

One particular strategy exemplifies this point: the use of state supplementation of SSI payments to assist in resource generation.[4]

Clearly, one of the most pressing problems facing state officials is the lack of out-of-home living arrangements, such as group homes and domiciliary units. One approach toward solving this shortage is to encourage the growth of privately operated (for profit or not) facilities, with state licensing standards and enforcement methods strengthened and expanded to cover these new facilities. SSI recipients must have sufficient resources, however, to stimulate interest in the private sector. The federal payments of $177.80 monthly through the SSI program are not sufficient to provide for the creation of new domiciliary facilities, nor will they provide for the whole range of needs of formerly institutionalized individuals.

This problem can be partially alleviated if the states supplement the federal payments for the target population. The additional cost to a state should not detract from the desirability of deinstitutionalization, since the state is already responsible for the financial support of institutionalizing these individuals. Although deinstitutionalization should not be undertaken merely because of potential cost savings, it should be stressed that the combination of SSI and associated benefits may be significantly less than the cost of institutional care previously borne by that state. Less intensive forms of care are usually less expensive, and the movement of eligible clients to the community can generate federal aid not available for those residing in institutions. This aid may offset the cost of additional state SSI supplementation in some instances.

In determining the amount of the supplement, the state should consider its value as an incentive in stimulating the desired growth of community-based facilities. The state may vary the amount of the supplement according to a number of factors, such as:

The level of supervision and the type of facility needed by the client

The number of facilities within the geographical area required to meet present and future needs

The category of recipient (aged, blind, or disabled)

To determine what the amount of this supplement should be, the state may take the following steps:

Estimate the number of people now institutionalized who could be cared for in community-based facilities

Determine the number of people that existing community-based facilities can support

Estimate the impact that each increment of SSI supplement will have on the supply and demand for community-based care units and identify the optimal supplemental amount

Estimate the cost of alternative supplemental amounts based on the data gathered in the first three steps and compare it with the amount that is to be saved in state institutional costs

Funding strategies such as this must be considered in the particular state context. An alternative to the above approach is to seek Title XIX support (ICF/MR) for small group living arrangements. Although only a few states have been successful in tailoring this program to small residences, state officials should not ignore the possibility. Minnesota and Connecticut, in particular, have funded several group homes under the program, and other states, such as Pennsylvania, are in the process of shifting their group homes to ICF/MR status.

Redeploy Institutional Resources

Whenever possible, it is desirable to eliminate or reduce less economical institutional settings in order to free funds for the expansion of community-based services. To date, however, few states have been able to realize savings in this way that can be redirected to meet the needs of clients in community settings. Pennsylvania is an example of a state that has tried unsuccessfully to reduce institutional costs despite a concerned deinstitutionalization initiative. This is in large part because the state has been plagued by increased federal staffing requirements, civil service obstacles, union opposition, and bureaucratic intransigence. For example, the state has been able to reduce the average daily institutional census from 10,598 to 8,397 from fiscal year 1972 to fiscal year 1977, a decrease of nearly 21 percent. Yet, at the same time, the authorized state institutional staffs have actually grown from 8,638 to 9,682, an increase of more than 12 percent. As a result, the annual cost per resident has tripled, going from $7,738 in fiscal year 1972 to $23,093 in fiscal year 1977. And with a declining census, federal aid has been reduced and the state has had to bear a proportionately greater share of the cost. On top of this, Pennsylvania has had to spend millions of dollars to improve its institutions in line with the federally mandated life-safety code and ICF/MR standards.

In order to maximize the savings that might be forthcoming from reductions in the institutional population, some states have focused their attention on one region or facility. Thus, a particular institution has been selected for increased community placements and intraregional transfers, so that significant portions of the facility can be phased-down or closed.

In many states, even where institutional savings have been possible, *they have reverted back to the state general fund with no provision for reappropriation to the community service network.* This is particularly the case in those states where institutional and community appropriations are separate. Massachusetts has resolved this problem in part by creating a "revolving" fund that can be used by state administrators to support institutional and community programs as the need arises. Called the 5016 account, this fund includes legislative appropriations for the staff necessary to bring the state's institutions for the mentally retarded up to federal standards. All such staff continue to be paid out of the 5016 account. If institutional populations decline, and the continued need for such staff is eliminated, the 5016 money can be transferred to priority areas in the community. California has established a similar system for transferring institutional savings in its mental health program. As county mental health agencies reduce their utilization of state hospitals, the state pays them a percentage of the savings in institutional cost per patient day.

Similarly, community providers in Canada who agree to accept developmentally disabled residents from the Alberta School and Hospital receive a *per diem* account comparable to the institutional rate adjusted for each individual's level of functioning.[5]

Since staff payrolls account for more than 80 percent of the cost of most services for developmentally disabled persons in institutional and community-based programs, any significant realignment of resources inevitably involves a corresponding shift in personnel. Efforts to transfer institutional staff to community programs, however, may encounter a number of roadblocks. In Pennsylvania, Iowa, and many other states, the institutional staff have salaries and accumulated benefits that cannot be matched by the proprietary and nonproprietary service providers in the community or by other prospective nonstate employers. As a result, many institutional staff, particularly those who are senior, resist transferring to nonstate positions where they may lose their superior salaries and benefits. Also, in many states institutional employees are unionized while their counterparts in the community are not. Thus, the unions fight employee transfers in the interest of their members and in the interest of maintaining the union membership. At the same time, nonstate providers resist accepting institutional staff on their payrolls, even when states offer to subsidize the higher salary and benefit levels that the providers must pay. They fear that hiring higher paid former state employees might lower the morale of their current employees, accelerate employee demands for higher pay, and hasten employee unionization.

A number of states have explored the desirability of permitting employees to transfer their state benefits to the counties or other local jurisdictions charged with administering community-based services. However, such proposals have generally been rejected by local officials, who fear that they would eventually lead to more costly and cumbersome local civil service systems.

To eliminate this problem among community living arrangement coordinators (CLACs) in Pennsylvania, the Office of Mental Retardation has kept the CLAC salaries at parity with the state salaries. Furthermore, a CLAC career ladder is being developed in the hope that it will serve as a further incentive to career-minded institutional staff who might consider relocating. Other states are circumventing this problem by "out-stationing" institutional staff in the community. In this way, staff are retained on state institutional payrolls but are assigned where needed in the community. Reportedly, a significant number of "out-stationed" staff grow to value their new assignments and are willing to forego their state positions in favor of permanent but less lucrative nonstate positions.

In Michigan, for example, the state institutions for the mentally retarded are responsible for supplying one full-time employee for each of twenty-five beds in nursing homes serving the mentally retarded. They are also responsible for supplying one full-time supervisor for each five full-time state employees assigned to these nursing home programs. These state employees are responsible for coordinating and assisting in specialized developmental and habilitative training programs for the mentally retarded residents. The institutions also provide backup consultation in nursing, education, and other skill areas that may be required. Finally, the institutions provide inservice education programs for nursing home personnel.

Still other states have largely avoided this problem. In California, the state and county civil service systems allow for transfer of benefits. In other states, such as North Carolina and Massachusetts, the state directly staffs the local administering agency.

Another factor that creates personnel problems is the relative isolation of many state facilities. Many state mental retardation institutions were purposefully constructed away from large communities and remain so today. As a result, the number of alternative employment opportunities available in the immediate area of the institutions are few. Institutional personnel who are unwilling or unable to relocate to other areas where job opportunities exist, may therefore be forced to resign or retire.

In the state of Washington, the Economic Impact Act was enacted to alleviate problems spawned by the closing of Northern State Hospital. The Act included state job guarantees, an early retirement option (which was elected by approximately one-third of the hospital employees), necessary employee retraining, and employee relocation allowances that include reimbursement for financial losses suffered upon the sale of their houses.[6]

Increase the Level of State Funding

Although other sources of funds can be used to assist in the development of resources, administrators and state officials should be aware that a substantial portion of the burden will always remain with the state. Many states have, indeed, accepted this fact over the past several years. For instance, California's total expenditures by all state agencies for services to the developmentally disabled, including preventive services, jumped to $335 million in fiscal year 1976, an increase of more than 20 percent in two years. In the past five years, Georgia's budget for day training centers for the mentally retarded has grown from $50,000 to over $25 million. In 1969, Nebraska spent $60,000 for community services for 85 clients, but by 1976 its expenditures were approximately $14 million for 3,000 clients. Pennsylvania's Family Resources Program has grown from $800,000 to $4 million, and its community living arrangements budget has gone from $2 million to nearly $15 million in the past two years. Moreover, in almost every state mentioned, state funds have been used to match additional federal funds, thereby expanding available monies for services two- and threefold.

Expand the Use of Generic Services

Another way to expand the resources available to developmentally disabled persons is to see that they gain access to generic services at the state and local levels. This can be done through client management, discussed in the fourth section of this chapter; through a local developmental disabilities agency; or through state-level interagency agreements.

In California, the regional centers for the developmentally disabled are responsible, among other things, for seeing that community agencies provide generic services to their clients. Although center staff may purchase services directly, they resist purchasing any service that is already available from another agency. In fact, this policy had to be reemphasized in recent months, as center staff were finding it easier to purchase certain services than to cajole another agency into meeting the need. The policy is now firm, however, and should result in a more aggressive posture with generic service providers.

Interagency arrangements between the DDA and other state agencies can substantially increase the availability of services. For instance, interagency agreements between the DDAs in Georgia and Connecticut and their state departments of education should eventually result in an expansion of educational programs for developmentally disabled children, a shift of the primary educational responsibility to the state departments of education, and a release of scarce developmental disability funds for other service priorities. Interagency agreements in other states have facilitated shifts of Title XX, Title XIX, and Vocational Rehabilitation funds to expanding community programs for the developmentally disabled.

Use Less Costly Alternatives

A final way to expand resources for the developmentally disabled is to invest in those services that minimize costs and maximize the likelihood of maintaining clients in the least restrictive program possible. Some of these services are family support services, family subsidies, and foster and adoptive placement programs, all of which are designed to enable clients to live in their communities without requiring the construction and staffing of residential facilities.

In Massachusetts, couples and single persons willing to share their homes with mentally retarded persons receive specialized training and approximately $350 per month to do so.[7] Training is provided for both the care providers and the individuals being placed. The program also provides allowances for special activities and job-training programs and pays for many support services, including respite care, medical and dental care, and various therapeutic and recreational programs.

In Pennsylvania,[8] Specialized Foster Family Services, a federally funded program operating at Cresson State School and Hospital, is successfully placing severely and profoundly retarded, multihandicapped children in foster homes. Once a child and family have been matched and the arrangement works to everyone's satisfaction, the project staff registers the child in a local school program. Specialized Foster Family Services provides all the necessary supportive services directly or through contracts with ancillary agencies.

Pennsylvania also provides an example of a program to support families with developmentally disabled children. Its Family Resource Services Program (FRS) was established to provide adequate resources within the community to allow natural or adoptive families with developmentally disabled family members to maintain them at home with minimal stress and disruption to the family. The services provided under the FRS program are:

Respite care This service makes a temporary residence available to a developmentally disabled person when his family is experiencing stress, personal crisis, or a need for a vacation

Family aide Family aides are provided for parents who need a person to care for their developmentally disabled family member for a few hours at a time

Homemaker services Homemakers may be available to perform essential household duties when family members are unable to manage such tasks effectively

Transportation This service may be offered to families who need assistance in transporting themselves, their child, or an adult family member to regular day programs or activity programs

Family education and training Programs may be offered to assist parents of developmentally disabled children, adult developmentally disabled individuals who are parents, or other family members in dealing with a family member who is developmentally disabled

Parents in Minnesota who keep their developmentally disabled child at home are eligible for a monthly subsidy of up to $250 under a law enacted by the state legislature during 1975.[9] To qualify for the program, the child must be under eighteen years of age and eligible for placement in a state institution or community residential facility. Once qualified, an individual program plan is written for the child with quarterly reviews by the Department of Public Welfare. The initial appropriation for the experimental project was $300,000. During the next two years, the progress of children in the program was closely monitored and compared with that of a similar group of institutional residents to determine if the family subsidy program was a feasible alternative to institutionalization.[10]

New York has a similar program under which families in New York City will receive $273.70 per month and up-state families will receive $218.70 per month. Before these payments can be received it must be determined that: (1) the family setting is consistent with the child's treatment plan; (2) the home setting meets the standards for all Department of Mental Health family care homes; and (3) the necessary support services are available.[11]

QUALITY ASSURANCE

As more and more developmentally disabled persons are diverted or released from institutions, the number of service agencies is also growing. In some states, the mushrooming of private nonprofit and proprietary service agencies has outpaced the states' ability to regulate them. This problem is a familiar one and is described in much of the literature. Abuses by nursing homes, board and care facilities, and other providers that have rushed to take up the institutional slack are an increasing concern to policymakers. At the same time, the quality of institutional facilities has come under increasing attack from consumers and public interest lawyers.

There are three major mechanisms available to states to ensure provider quality and responsiveness. One is licensing, the process of legally designating those facilities that are empowered to provide services to particular groups of clients. A second is standard setting, the development of programmatic criteria by which potential service providers may be evaluated. The third is rate setting, the process of establishing reimbursement rates for officially sanctioned services. In order to ensure provider compliance with each aspect, the state must also establish an enforcement mechanism.

Regulation of providers has several objectives within the context of system reform. These are:

To ensure each client's well-being and safety
To stimulate the creation of services that are responsive to the needs of the developmentally disabled
To ensure that services are delivered in an economical and efficient fashion
To guarantee consistency in the quality of services provided across the state

An important dilemma in the regulation of providers is how far out to cast the state net. For instance, should the state develop certification procedures for proprietary board and care facilities even though the clientele of such facilities is generally nonhandicapped? Conversely, should a legally competent developmentally disabled person be prevented from residing in a facility of his or her choice if it is not state certified? The breadth of regulation is also significant because of the added monitoring burden that it entails.

Before adopting quality assurance regulations, state officials should also be aware of the conflict between institutional and community-based standards when resources are scarce. By setting institutional standards at an optimal level, the state ultimately faces a funding priority question. If sufficient resources are diverted to the institutions to substantially improve the quality of care, it is fairly safe to assume that funding to develop services at the community level will suffer.

Licensing

Licensing is becoming an increasingly complex task in decentralized systems of care for the developmentally disabled. In many states, unless the number of licensing officials at the state level is increased to reflect the growth in the number of facilities licensed, the states' ability to conduct on-site reviews will become negligible. If the states are unwilling to commit additional resources to this purpose, then other possibilities must be explored. One such possibility is delegation of inspection or licensing certification to local government or to regional developmental disabilities authorities.

To maintain the responsiveness and integrity of the licensing function, it is important to keep the following in mind:

To the extent possible, licensing should be centralized at the state level to ensure continuity of requirements and jurisdictions

Licensing requirements should be reviewed periodically to ensure their relevance to the services so regulated

Physical facility requirements should serve to enhance rather than constrain the programmatic mission of the agency or residence

Licensing requirements should be developed with the assistance of provider and consumer review to assure that they are consistent with both administrative and quality-of-life concerns

Standard Setting

Standard setting is closely related to licensing but is concerned more with scope and quality of services offered by an agency than the physical structure in which they are offered. Standard setting is that aspect of quality control that most directly affects the content of services for developmentally disabled persons. This puts an affirmative responsibility on the designers of new standards to become knowledgable regarding recent advances in the state of the art.

Developing standards that will facilitate achievement of the goals of system reform is difficult. Traditionally standards have dealt primarily with structural and safety concerns. Many of these structural constraints are more appropriate to institutional settings and severely hamper the smaller provider's ability to establish a homelike and nonstigmatizing atmosphere. So that program standards facilitate the development of a balanced system, the following should be noted:

Standards should address the relationship between program content and the levels of functioning of the clients served

Standards should include some level of expectation regarding provider performance

Standards should be reviewed periodically to ensure that they have kept pace with changing programmatic concepts

Proposed standards should be reviewed by providers and consumers

Standards should be consistent with the principles of normalization, including age and disability appropriateness

Development of Rates

Rate setting, although not strictly a control on program quality, can assist or constrain the development of adequate services. The influence that rates have on the availability of services is particularly apparent in states that rely on purchase-of-service arrangements. Because these systems are dependent on the marketplace to supply services, the attractiveness of the financial "carrot" that is held out is all important.

The establishment of rates should take into consideration the following:

Rates should be flexible enough to accommodate a variety of program components and combinations because of the range of services required by developmentally disabled persons

Rates should be reviewed periodically to ensure their consistency with changing economic conditions

Rates should provide incentives rather than dis-incentives for the development of less restrictive modes of care

The accounting process required to determine rates should be consistent with the budgeting requirements of various relevant federal funding programs

Multiple rate-setting and regulatory bodies have heightened the confusion created by decentralization of services. Many local facilities, because they serve a clientele that is referred from a variety of human service agencies, must in some instances meet two or more sets of licensing or certification standards. In addition to standards imposed by the state and local governing bodies, physical or programmatic restrictions may also be imposed by planning commissioners, building inspectors, and others. The problem of multiple regulatory agencies is compounded in some states with overlapping rate-setting authorities. Again, because agencies may receive clients from more than one source, they may also be subject to more than one reimbursement schedule.

In some states, health, welfare, mental health, mental retardation, and juvenile justice agencies all have their own rate-setting mechanisms. These conflicting jurisdictions may have significant impact on the ability of the developmental disabilities system to compete for resources. If other agencies are offering levels of reimbursement that are higher than those set by the DDA, then the ability of the authority to secure needed placements may be severely undercut.

Similarly, if other state agencies are setting standards for facilities utilized by the DDA, then there is likely to be some question as to the responsiveness of such standards to the client group in question. Conversely, if developmentally disabled persons are to be encouraged to participate in more generic and less specialized programs, then standards should be sufficiently flexible to accommodate them.

California, through legislation passed a few years ago, has attempted to resolve the multiple licensing authority problem at the state level. State law unifies previously separate licensing functions into one licensing body under the Department of Health. The provisions of the act require the development of generic categories of facilities and a scheme of program components or "add-ons" that can be certified according to the types of clients being served. This approach also makes it possible to determine rates based on the configuration of specialized program elements built on the foundation of generic services.

Enforcement

Enforcement is an overriding concern in the area of quality control and is possibly the most difficult component to design. Although enforcement is in part a function of the precision and utility of the facility and program standards, it is also an administrative matter requiring the maximization of scarce personnel resources. The following principles should guide enforcement:

- Abridgement of quality control standards should be punishable by strict sanctions spelled out in statute and regulation
- Clients and their families should be given an opportunity to air grievances regarding the services rendered
- State agencies should explore the possibility of delegating some enforcement responsibilities to local government or private, nonprofit agencies

COORDINATED CLIENT MANAGEMENT SYSTEM

Of the four basic implementation requirements, the element that is probably most critical to the welfare of the individual developmentally disabled person is a coordinated client management system. At best, a weak system invites discontinuity between clients and resources, and at worst it may result in actual abuse and exploitation of vulnerable persons. An effective client management system can serve as a buffer between the individual and the more confusing and irrational elements in the delivery system.

The development of a client management system is directly relevant to primary goals such as integration of developmentally disabled persons into community living arrangements, the creation of diagnostic and evaluation procedures that lead to individual assessments and treatment plans, the placement of clients in settings that meet their needs and represent the least restrictive alternative, and the participation of developmentally disabled persons and their families in the preparation of their service plans. To the extent that client management also contributes to quality control (through the monitoring component), it also can assist in the attainment of full and equal rights for the developmentally disabled, the elimination of harmful or exploitative residential environments, and ready access to generic services.

To date, most states have not established a comprehensive, accountable client management system, but have relied on fragmentary support from social work staff in the institutions, local social service workers, aftercare workers in individual agencies, vocational rehabilitation counselors, and mental health workers. None of these groups can be held accountable for the client's total well-being, and the failure to do so invites buck-passing and nonproductive territorial squabbles.

This problem has been addressed most directly by California, which, through its regional center network, has a unified client management system based in twenty-one regional centers for the developmentally disabled. Case workers at the regional centers are responsible for each client's welfare from the point at which he or she enters the system to the point at which the client is believed to be capable of living independently without supervision.

One general constraint that seems to impede the creation of a responsive and accountable client management process is the notion that an eventual integration of human services will obviate the need for categorical client monitoring systems. It is feared, therefore, that the establishment of such systems will delay the eventual integration of human services. This argument ignores the significant body of information that client managers for the developmentally disabled can provide (e.g., information regarding gaps and discontinuities in services) to support such eventual integration.

Client management also entails some internal contradictions that limit its effectiveness. On the one hand, its purpose is to protect the client's well-being, but it also entails a form of "surveillance" that in some ways limits the rights of the individual to privacy and free choice. Understanding this should assist client managers in making important distinctions between protecting a client's freedom of choice and assuring necessary professional intervention on his behalf. Even in cases where the client is under some protective jurisdiction, it is important to preserve his or her basic rights to the extent possible.

As a process, client management has the following specific objectives:

To focus responsibility and accountability for the client's well-being

To ensure continuity among care providers (e.g., community facilities and state institutions)

To assist in the development of linkages between the client and generic human services agencies

To assess and document the gaps in services and the obstacles that prevent developmentally disabled persons from securing generic and specialized services

To accomplish these ends, client management should include diagnosis and evaluation, individual planning and referral, predischarge planning, monitoring and follow-up, and client advocacy. The client management process begins when the client enters the system and continues as long as the client is in need of services or supervision. These functions do not necessarily have to be performed by the same agency, but should be linked by formal, structural arrangements.

Client management is not a panacea, especially when it involves no more than a perfunctory visit to the client every several months. But it can, when effectively organized, provide the glue necessary to bind together a diverse array of services on behalf of developmentally disabled persons. The following sections describe each element of client management, problems of implementing such systems, and examples of particular approaches.

Diagnosis and Evaluation

Diagnosis and evaluation can be generally categorized as "intake" functions. They are particularly important since they constitute the client's initial experience with the system of care. It is at this point that the developmentally disabled person is assessed and decisions are made concerning admission and the future provision of service. The principal components are case finding (outreach), screening, and assessment.

These elements have direct relevance to the achievement of system reform. The outreach portion of the process is crucial to successful early intervention, which, in turn, may help to prevent the need for institutionalization in many cases. If problems are identified at an early stage, it may be possible to intervene with an intensive service program that will result in an amelioration of the client's disability. The screening portion of this initial phase is important as it is crucial to direct clients away from unnecessary institutional care into more appropriate community settings. Careful screening and client assessment provide assurance that developmentally disabled persons receive care appropriate to their needs.

Individual client assessments can also be viewed as building blocks in the larger needs assessment process. Over time, the aggregate of these client "work-ups" can be useful in determining the number of developmentally disabled persons, their geographical distribution, and, when coupled with service-needs information, the demand for services and the adequacy of available resources. These data should assist planners in identifying the risk populations and in determining priorities for those services most likely to diminish such risk.

Several major elements are generally agreed to characterize an effective and efficient intake process. They are:

A single entry point, in the community, for developmentally disabled persons and their families who seek services
An active outreach program that is geared to identifying unserved and underserved developmentally disabled persons
An array of assessment procedures that measure each client's level of functioning
A multidisciplinary assessment team
The involvement of the client and guardian, as appropriate, in the development of the initial assessment

The creation of a single entry point is particularly important for states striving to integrate intake, individualized planning, and service procurement. A number of states, including Pennsylvania and California, have attempted such integration at the local level. The former has identified "base service units" at the county or sub-county level as the service entry point for developmentally disabled citizens. California, on the other hand, has established twenty-one regional centers that serve as the initial point of contact between clients and the publicly supported system for developmentally disabled persons.

Even when a state has developed an integrated system of entry services in the community, it can still be circumvented by the courts. In the early seventies, Pennsylvania closed admissions to one of its major state schools for the mentally retarded in an effort to halt overcrowding and to concentrate its efforts on reducing the institutional population. Although admissions were substantially reduced, the courts were still able to make institutional placements when they deemed them appropriate. This points up the importance of reforming involuntary commitment provisions at the same time that steps are being taken to halt or reduce admissions to large institutions.

Individual Service Planning

Individual service planning involves the development of individualized treatment and habilitation plans. The importance of preparing such plans is reinforced in a growing number of comprehensive court orders in right-to-treatment cases and in the recent amendments to the Developmental Disabilities Act.

Once the diagnostic and evaluation phases of client intake are completed, the next step is the development of an individual plan of services that meets the client's needs. The plan represents a comprehensive statement of all the service interventions (generic and specialized) that the client will require over a specified period of time. Each individualized treatment plan should be reviewed at appropriate junctures to determine the extent of client progress and whether the prescribed services continue to be relevant. Furthermore, it can serve as a useful resource for outside reviewers who are evaluating service quality.

The major elements of individualized planning and service procurement include:

Involvement of the client and guardian, where appropriate, in planning and goal setting

Establishment of short- and long-term goals that are achievable, reasonable, and measurable
Identification of client strengths, as well as weaknesses, that can be built upon during the habilitation process
Designation of accountable staff and the agencies responsible for carrying out various facets of the plan

To ensure that agencies prepare habilitation plans on a regular basis, they should be mandated to do so by statute or regulation. Illinois, for instance, has recently issued guidelines that require an individualized habilitation or treatment plan for every resident in a state facility. The new provisions, which resulted from a court case (*Nathan v. Levitt*), require the preparation of an initial plan within twenty-two hours of admission and, after fourteen days, preparation of a revised plan that is to be reevaluated and modified as necessary every month thereafter.[12]

Unfortunately, inadequate knowledge of available services often impedes this phase of client management, as well as the others which follow. If a client's plan is to include the full array of services required, then case workers must be familiar with specialized as well as generic services. In practice, however, territorial and functional boundaries often prevent workers from gaining such familiarity.

Service Procurement

The development of an individualized plan should be followed immediately by a process of identification and procurement of available services to meet the plan requirements. This stage of the client management process is particularly important to the achievement of the integration of services and placement of clients in the least restrictive settings available. Additionally, the intervention of the client manager at this stage of the process enhances the probability of appropriate service placement, establishes the necessary linkages among service providers, and ensures that the client and his or her family will not be left at the mercy of an uncoordinated system.

There are a number of ways that this function may be carried out. In some instances, the case manager may refer clients to other agencies in the community according to some prearranged agreement. In others, the case manager may be empowered to purchase services on behalf of the client from community providers. In still others, the case manager may place the client into a service run directly by his or her agency, although it is argued that this latter arrangement places the referral agent in a conflict-of-interest position.

Each of these modes of service procurement has characteristic strengths and weaknesses. The initial form, referral to existing services, may suffer from the case worker's inability to ensure that referrals in fact result in appropriate treatment. Ordinarily, the case worker must rely on the apparent good will of the agencies since he or she usually has little or no ability to force them to respond to the needs of the client.

The second form of service procurement, purchase of services, gives the case manager a stronger hand, since he or she has funds with which to shop for services. Yet this "checkbook" power provides no assurance that the service marketplace can in fact supply the services that the client needs. The purchase-of-service mechanism is premised upon the assumption that the availability of funds will encourage the development of needed services, but the availability of funds is not the only variable that influences the supply of services. Other factors such as rates of reimbursement, the terms of federal regulations, the availability of trained personnel, and the state of the art also influence the development of services needed by clients.

The third form of service procurement, provision of direct services, avoids the problems encountered in the purchase of service system since it allows the worker to place clients in tailor-made services developed by the primary agency. But although this may encourage responsiveness to client needs, it places the case worker in a less than objective position. Being employed by the providing agency, the case worker may find it difficult to be critical of the agency's programs or to recognize the client's legitimate need for alternative services.

In any case, the location, procurement, and provision of services should proceed from established goals and objectives set for the client. To ensure the relevance of these goals, they should be reviewed periodically to determine the need for additional or alternative services. And the client and his or her family should participate in the development and review of these goals to the greatest extent possible.

Predischarge Planning

Predischarge planning involves the preparation of a client for transfer from a more restrictive to a less restrictive environment.

Such a move may be from a large institution to a community living arrangement, from a group home to a supervised apartment, and so forth. Intervention at this point is particularly important since the client is moving to a more independent lifestyle, and adequate planning may make the difference between success and failure in the new setting.

Predischarge planning entails an assessment of the client's level of functioning, identification of the less restrictive living arrangements that are available to the client, and creation of a transitional training program to ensure that the client develops the skills that will be required in his or her new environment. The task of predischarge planning can be performed by the institution in which the client currently resides, by the staff of the program to which the client is being transferred, or by an independent case management agency. In some states, portions of this function may be carried out by all three.

Factors that contribute to the success of predischarge planning include:

Establishment of close ties between predischarge planners and potential service providers
Involvement of potential community providers in the client's predischarge transitional program
Involvement of the client and guardian, where appropriate, in the selection of service and residential settings
Creation of transitional programs that assist the client in developing skills that will be necessary in the succeeding placement

Unfortunately, institutional staff are often at a disadvantage in attempting to develop effective transitional programs for clients transferring to community settings. Recent research with long-term institutional residents suggests that skills developed in an institutional setting are not necessarily transferrable to community living and working environments. Severely disabled persons, especially, require training that is directly relevant to their new circumstances (e.g., how to shop, cook for themselves, and use public transportation), which is difficult to duplicate in institutional surroundings.

Planning for a client's transition to the community is hampered, also, if the staff of the institution is unfamiliar with available resources in the community in which the client is to be placed. There appear to be few states that have mounted comprehensive inservice training programs to inform client managers about the types of entitlements and community services available to their clients.

In addition to facilitating the successful transfer of clients to community living, a skilled client manager is in a position to identify the service gaps, constraints, and resistances that confront the clients in the generic service system. This information is crucial to policy-makers seeking to make such services more accessible. To ensure the participation of all interested agencies in the client management process, some states have created mechanisms for multiple agency participation. Michigan, for example, has established a prerelease review team comprised of representatives of all relevant agencies. This team deliberates on placement issues and assigns responsibility for clients to community agencies on a case-by-case basis.

Monitoring and Follow-up

Once the client has been assessed and services have been secured, the next step in the case management process is monitoring and follow-up to ensure that the client's needs are being met. Monitoring and follow-up serve a number of purposes directly relevant to reform aims. Continuing attention to each client's needs ensures that the initial individualized plan is updated as new or modified services are required. It also provides a form of protection for the client against abuse and exploitation. Beyond this, regular monitoring and follow-up provide a means for assessing the quality of services provided and for collecting data on client progress that can be valuable in determining the effectiveness of various services.

To carry out an effective monitoring and follow-up activity, the following elements should be present:

Availability of sanctions enabling case workers to upgrade services on behalf of clients

Caseloads that are sufficiently small to allow the client manager time to conduct periodic checks on each client's status

Reevaluation of each client's needs to ensure the continuing appropriateness of the service plan

Collection of client progress data to ensure service responsiveness

Because many developmentally disabled persons have handicaps that require at least intermittent attention over the course of their lifetimes, case monitoring and follow-up should also be lifelong. For the client management agency, this means a constantly growing caseload for the first several years of operation, at least. Some agencies have handled this problem by closing cases in which no foreseeable intervention is required; others eventually move cases to an "inactive" status. Since one of the major goals for developmentally disabled persons is maximization of independence and individual choice, the closure of client cases until and if additional needs arise seems preferable.

The issue of sanctions is also important. If client managers are to make a realistic contribution to quality control and if case managers are to be successful advocates for their clients, then realistic sanctions should be developed that can be used against recalcitrant agencies. States that use purchase-of-service methods of obtaining service, such as California, have a built-in sanction: they can threaten to terminate an agency's funding if it does not provide an adequate level of service.

Advocacy

Advocacy is probably the most loosely defined of all the elements of client management. Clearly, every volunteer, professional, parent, and administrator considers himself or herself to be an advocate for developmentally disabled persons. In the broad sense they are. However, recent amendments to the Developmental Disabilities Act have forced states to define the term "advocate" narrowly.[13] The new provisions require the states, as a condition of continued funding under the Act, to establish advocacy programs for developmentally disabled persons. These programs must:

Have the authority to pursue legal, administrative, and other appropriate remedies to ensure the protection of the rights of all developmentally disabled persons who are receiving treatment, services, or habilitation within the state

Be independent of any state agency that provides treatment, services, or habilitation to persons with developmental disabilities

This language makes it quite clear that to qualify as an advocacy system that is free of conflicts of interest, the proposed program must be separate from the regular delivery system. This separateness also protects the advocacy system from being assigned client management functions that should be the responsibility of the state developmental disabilities authority or other agencies.

It is evident that Congress sees the advocacy system as an entity that represents the client alone in his or her struggle to secure services and entitlements. This does not necessarily place the new advocacy system in a competing role with other client management functions. Instead, it should provide the necessary back-up resources for the client manager who is unable to secure services from a reluctant agency. Similarly, client managers can provide valuable information to advocates and can be of assistance in pointing out priority needs for intervention or litigation.

NOTES

1. See Human Services Research Institute, *An Evaluation of the Mental Health Pilot Project in the Northeast Region of Pennsylvania,* January 31, 1978 (mimeographed).
2. At least 80 percent of the residents of CLAs must be from a state institution.
3. For purposes of this report, the "service network" is defined as the spectrum of residential and support services necessary to maintain a developmentally disabled person in the least restrictive and most integrated environment feasible. The network, in order to accommodate all levels of functioning, must include residential and service environments ranging from twenty-four hour supervision to support for independent living. It must be sufficiently diverse to include programs for a wide variety of client needs, including shelter, income maintenance, transportation, self-help and vocational skill development, social and cultural activities, and education. Much of this service network does not have to be created anew. Rather, existing generic services should be intertwined with specialized agencies so that all available resources are utilized. It is the lack of such meshing that enforces the continued isolation of developmentally disabled citizens.
4. This discussion of the use of SSI is excerpted from an unpublished article by Tom Joe, of Lewin and Associates, Inc., entitled "Some Perspectives on Human Services Program Development," a monograph prepared for the School of Social Service Administration, University of Chicago, July 1974, p. 7.
5. National Association of Coordinators for State Programs for the Mentally Retarded, Inc., *New Directions,* March 1977. For additional information contact: Dr. R. Short, Director, Services for the Handicapped, Social Services and Community Health, South Tower, Petroleum Plaza, 9915-108 Street, Edmonton, Alberta, Canada.

6. Program Development Department, American Federation of State, County and Municipal Employees, *Deinstitutionalization Manual,* 1975.
7. For additional information contact: Specialized Home Care Program, Department of Mental Health, 190 Portland Street, Boston, Massachusetts 02114. Source: *New Directions,* April 1977.
8. For additional information contact: Marian Wikramanayake, Coordinator, Specialized Foster Family Services, P.O. Box 81, Cresson, Pennsylvania 16630. Source: *New Directions,* April 1977.
9. Minnesota Statute 252.27.
10. For additional information contact: Thomas Coughlin, Deputy Commissioner for Mental Retardation, 44 Holland Avenue, Albany, New York 12229. Source: *New Directions,* January 1976.
11. For additional information contact: Warren Bock, Assistant Director, Mental Retardation Program Office, Department of Public Welfare, Centennial Office Building, St. Paul, Minnesota 55155. Source: *New Directions,* January 1976.
12. Reevaluations must include: (1) a description of the review process and staff participants, (2) any changes in the client's level of functioning, (3) proposed modifications and the justification, and (4) target dates for completion of each phase of the plan. Source: *New Directions,* May, 1976, pp. 12–13.
13. Developmental Disabilities Assistance and Bill of Rights Act of 1975 (PL 94-103), Section 113.

SUMMARY
Chapter five

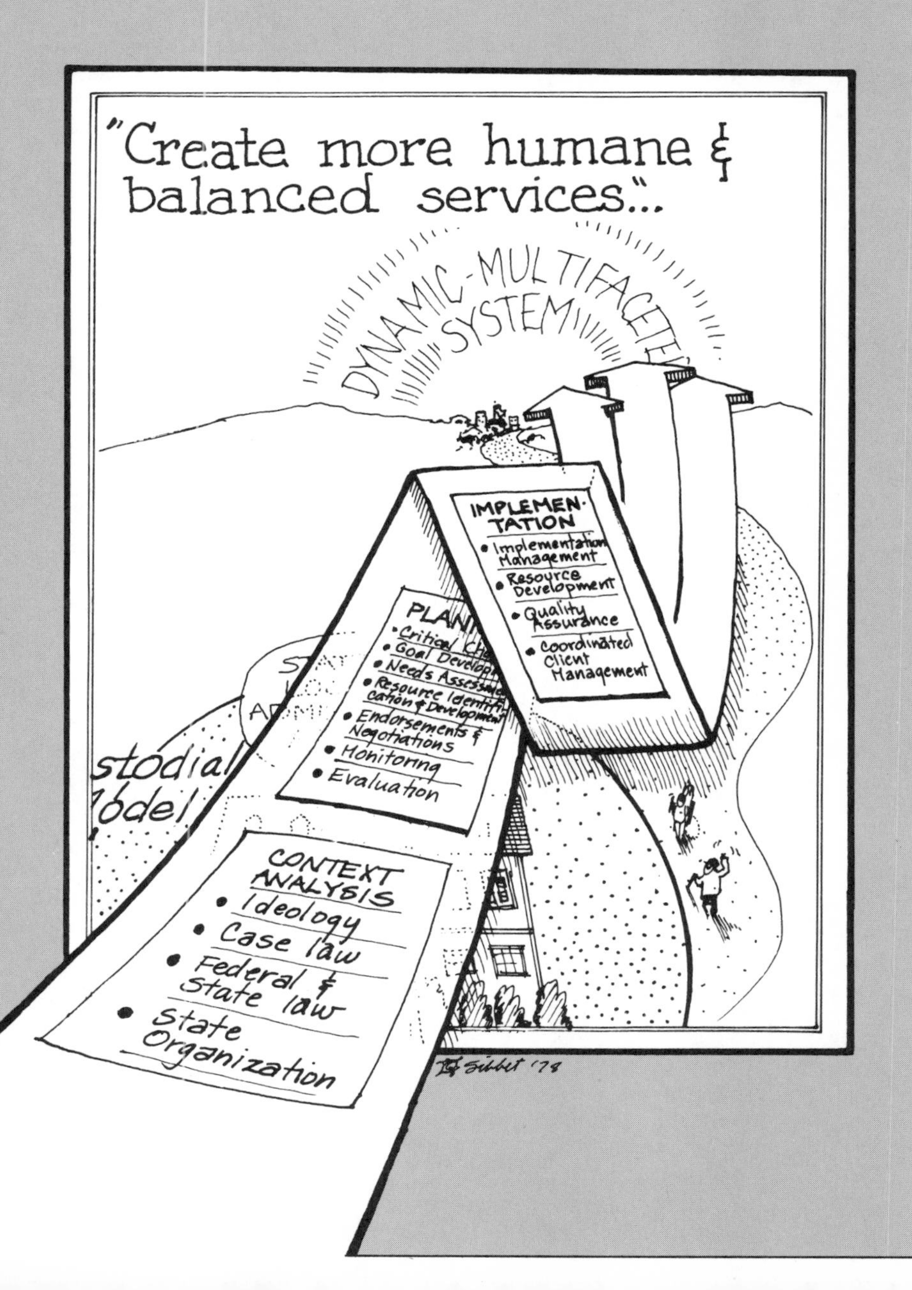

The results of attempts to create a more humane and balanced system of services for developmentally disabled persons by moving many of them out of large custodial institutions and into community-based programs have mainly been incremental and, in some states, inconclusive. These attempts have suffered most seriously from the lack of an integrated vision of the multiple steps required to bring about systematic reform in this field. Reform efforts to date have not been sufficiently comprehensive, owing in large part to the short (though intensive) history of the reform movement and the normal lag between the development of new program concepts and their general acceptance among state and local officials and the public.

The erratic nature of reform efforts in some states has, unfortunately, created stresses and strains on the delivery of services to developmentally disabled persons. Among these are:

Inappropriate community placements that result in exploitation of the client and, in some instances, his or her return to an institution

Anxiety among the parents and families of developmentally disabled persons who reside in institutions because they fear that the state may abdicate responsibility for their family member

Continued competition for funds between institutional and community programs, a fact that has been aggravated by the impact of new federal regulations requiring significant improvements in institutional care

Inadequate fiscal and other incentives to encourage the development of the full array of resources required in the community to meet the needs of the developmentally disabled

These and other problems will continue to plague state efforts at system improvement until the entire context in which these changes must take place is taken into consideration. This includes all of the factors that have a direct bearing on how services are delivered—those that are within the power of state officials to control and those that are not. These factors include the values and policies that motivate system improvement, the recent judicial mandates stressing client rights, each state's administrative and political structure, and the numerous federal health and welfare programs that provide support for services for developmentally disabled persons.

This analysis must in turn be followed by the creation of a comprehensive plan that sets goals for the system, anticipates the impact of the various external variables already assessed, estimates the magnitude of need among developmentally disabled persons, creates strategies for resource development, establishes benchmarks for goal achievement, and delegates responsibility for specific implementation tasks. In preparing this plan, it is also important that responsible state administrators secure its endorsement by elected officials and the major interest groups that influence policy in the field of developmental disabilities.

Finally, there are four basic elements of the implementation process that together are the *sine qua non* of efforts to achieve the goals outlined in the plan. They are: creation of implementation management units solely responsible for carrying out various objectives in the plan, a concerted resource development process to ensure availability of needed services, development of quality assurance procedures to guarantee provider compliance, and a client management structure to assist developmentally disabled persons in moving from one component of the service system to another.

Although many problems have arisen regarding the implementation of needed changes in this field, the authors feel optimistic that this more comprehensive and integrated approach will, when followed carefully, eliminate most of the major obstacles to effective system reform. To carry it out, however, state officials, administrators, and service providers must commit themselves to an intensive and demanding transitional phase in which the system will change from one that is dominated by large institutions to one that provides a more balanced system of care and habilitation. It is, of course, the resulting improvement in conditions for developmentally disabled citizens that will make this commitment worthwhile.

APPENDIX I
Bibliography

A. GENERAL DISCUSSION OF MENTAL RETARDATION, DEVELOPMENTAL DISABILITIES, DEINSTITUTIONALIZATION, AND INSTITUTIONS AND SERVICE DELIVERY

Acuff, Charles E. *Alternatives in the Delivery of Service to the Developmentally Disabled.* Birmingham, Ala.: Management Training Program, Center for Developmental and Learning Disorders, University of Alabama, undated.

American Federation of State, County and Municipal Employees. *Out of Their Beds and Into the Streets,* 1975.

Bachrach, Leona. *Deinstitutionalization: An Analytical Review and Sociological Perspective* (Draft Report). Washington, D.C.: National Institute of Mental Health, 1976.

Balla, David A., Mark McCormik, and Edward Zigler. Resident care practice in institutions for retarded persons: A cross-institutional, cross-cultural study. *American Journal of Mental Deficiency,* 1975, 80(1), 1–7.

Balla, David A., Mark McCormick, and Edward Zigler. Relationship of institution size to quality of care: A review of the literature. *American Journal of Mental Deficiency,* 1976, 81(2), 117–124.

Begab, Michael, and Stephen Richardson (eds.). *The Mentally Retarded and Society: A Social Science Perspective.* Baltimore: University Park Press, 1975.

Bogdan, Robert. *Observing in Institutions.* Syracuse, N.Y.: Center on Human Policy, 1974.

Braddock, David. *Trend Analysis of Administrative Documents Pertinent to the Community Alternatives and Institutional Reform Planning Grant Program,* 1975.

Braddock, David. *Opening Closed Doors: The Deinstitutionalization of Disabled Individuals.* Reston, Va.: Council for Exceptional Children, 1977.

Butterfield, Earl C. Institutionalization and its alternatives. Paper presented at University of Kansas Medical Center, September 1976.

Copeland, William. Discussion of the problem of deinstitutionalization (Draft Paper). 1976.

Datel, William E., and Murphy, Jane G. Service integrating model for deinstitutionalization. *Administration and Mental Health,* 1975, 4, 35–45.

Goldman, Edward R. A state model for community services. *Mental Retardation,* October 1975, 13(4), 33–36.

Goldman, Edward R. *Community services: The only salvation of deinstitutionalization.* Birmingham, Ala.: Management Training Program, Center for Developmental and Learning Disorders, University of Alabama, 1976.

Halpern, A., K. Fox, and J. Nagle. *A Planning and Evaluation Strategy for State Developmental Disabilities Councils: Progress Report.* Eugene, Ore.: Rehabilitation Research and Training Center in Mental Retardation, University of Oregon, 1973.

Halpern, A., K. Fox, and J. Farah. *A Planning and Evaluation Strategy for State Developmental Disabilities Councils* (Vol. 2). Eugene, Ore.: Rehabilitation Research and Training Center in Mental Retardation, University of Oregon, 1974.

Hobbs, Nicholas (ed.). *Issues in the Classification of Children* (Vols. 1 and 2). San Francisco: Jossey-Bass, 1975.

Horizon House Institute for Research and Development. *Proceedings of a Conference on Creating the Community Alternative: Options and Innovations.* Philadelphia: Horizon House Institute for Research and Development, 1974.

Jackson, Jay. The Jackson way: Four community agencies unite to serve developmentally disabled. *Tennessee Mental Health,* 1974, 11(4), 7–9.

Karls, Jane M. Retraining hospital staff for work in community programs in California. *Hospital and Community Psychiatry,* 1970, 27(4), 263–265.

Levitt, Leroy P. Deinstitutionalization: Accomplishments, issues and directions. Paper presented at the National Conference on Social Welfare, Washington, D.C., June 1976.

Litton, Freddie W., and James L. Sartin. Developmental disabilities 1970–1974. *Journal of Developmental Disabilities,* 1974, 1(1), 3–8.

Luckey, Robert E., and Ronald S. Newman. The President's Panel Recommendations—Today. *Mental Retardation,* 1975, 13(8), 32–34.

Martin, G. The future for the severely and profoundly retarded: Institutionalization? Normalization? Kinkare? Foster homes? *Canadian Psychologist,* 15(3), 1974.

Menolascino, Frank J., and Paul H. Pearson (eds.). *Beyond the Limits: Innovations in Services for the Severely and Profoundly Retarded.* Seattle, Wash.: Special Child Publications, 1974.

Neufeld, G. R. *Deinstitutionalization Procedures.* Chapel Hill, N.C.: DDTA System, University of North Carolina, 1976.

Pettinelli, Vincent D. Deinstitutionalization begins with the institution. *New Mandate,* 1974, 2(2), 7.

President's Committee on Mental Retardation. *Report to the President 1976: Mental Retardation, Century of Decision,* 1976.

Program Development Department, American Federation of State, County and Municipal Employees. *Deinstitutionalization Manual,* 1975.

Rosen, M. Independence for the mentally retarded. *Intellect,* 1975, 103, 35–37.

Ross, E. Clarke. *Trends in Federal Programming for the Severely Disabled: Impact on Local and State Service Agencies.* Washington, D.C.: United Cerebral Palsy Association, 1976.

Scheerenberger, R. C. *A Realistic Model for Deinstitutionalization.* Birmingham, Ala.: Management Training Program, Center for Development and Learning Disorders, University of Alabama, 1974.

Scheerenberger, R. C. A study of public residential facilities. *Mental Retardation,* 1976, 13(1), 32–35.

Segal, Robert. Current trends in the delivery of services to the mentally retarded. *Mental Retardation,* 1971, 9(1), 44–47.

Stedman, Donald J. The state planning and advisory council on developmental disabilities. *Mental Retardation,* 1975, 13(3), 4–8.
Stein, Leonard, and Mary Ann Ist. Retraining hospital staff for work in a community program in Wisconsin. *Hospital and Community Psychiatry.* 1976, 27(4), 266–268.
Thurman, K., and R. Thiele. A viable role for retardation institutions: The road to self-destruction. *Mental Retardation,* 1973, 2(2), 21–22.
U.S. Rehabilitation Services Administration. *The SID Report* (Vols. 1–8). Washington, D.C.: U.S. Government Printing Office, 1975.
Wolfensberger, W. Will there always be an institution? The impact of epidemiological trends. *Mental Retardation,* 1971, 12(6), 14–20.
Wolfensberger, Wolf. *Normalization: The Principle of Normalization in Human Services.* Toronto, Can.: National Institute on Mental Retardation, 1972.
Wolfensberger, Wolf. Will there always be an institution? The impact of new service models. *Mental Retardation,* 1974, 9(5), 31–37.

B. COMMUNITY-BASED ISSUES

Residential Care, Support Services, Evaluation and Zoning

Baker, Bruce, Gary B. Seltzer, and Marsha M. Seltzer. *As Close As Possible: A Study of Community Residences for Retarded Adults.* Cambridge, Mass.: Harvard University Press, 1974.
Bangs, Frank S., and Daniel Lauber. *Zoning for Family and Group Care Facilities, Planning Advisory Service Reports.* Chicago: The American Society of Planning Officials, 1974.
Bass, Rosalyn. A method for measuring continuity of care in a community mental health center. *NIMH Mental Health Statistics,* Series C, no. 4, 1972.
Bergman, Joel. *Community Homes for the Retarded.* Lexington, Ky.: D.C. Heath, 1975.
Birenbaum, A. Resettling mentally retarded adults in the community. *Intellect,* 1975, 103, 443–446.
Butterfield, Earl C. Basic changes in residential facilities for mentally retarded. *Changing Patterns in Residential Services for the Mentally Retarded.* Washington, D.C.: President's Committee on Mental Retardation, 1976.
Chandler, Jo Ann L., and Sterling Ross, Jr. Zoning barriers to normalization. Draft paper, President's Committee on Mental Retardation, undated.
Cherington, Carolyn, and Gunner Dybwod (eds.). *New Neighbors: The Retarded Citizen in Quest of a Home.* Washington, D.C.: President's Committee on Mental Retardation, 1974.
The Clover Bottom Development Center plan of action: Services provided to the mentally retarded: Pattern for change. *Breakthrough,* 1975, 33, 8–11.

Collins, Malcolm J., and Doris H. Rodman. A residential program for the developmentally disabled. *Social Work,* 1974, 19(6), 724–726.

Dempsey, John (ed.). *Community Services for Retarded Children: The Consumer–Provider Relationship.* Baltimore: University Park Press, 1975.

Fanning, John. *A Common Sense Approach to Community Living Arrangements for the Mentally Retarded.* Springfield, Ill.: Charles C Thomas, 1975.

Fields, Suzanne. Asylum on the front porch. I: Community life for the mentally retarded. *Innovations,* 1974, 1(4), 11–18.

Freedman, Ruth, Elinor Gollay, and Marty Wyngaarden. *A Study of Community Adjustment of Deinstitutionalized Mentally Retarded Persons.* Vol. IV: *Executive Summary: Findings and Recommendations.* Washington, D.C.: Bureau of Education for the Handicapped, 1976.

Glenn, Linda, and Wolf Wolfensberger. *Program Analysis of Service Systems. (PASS): A Method for the Quantitative Evaluation of Human Services.* Ontario, Can.: York University National Institute on Mental Retardation, 1975.

Grossman, Frances Kaplan, Seymour B. Sarason, and George Zitnay. *The Creation of a Community Setting.* New York: Syracuse University Division of Special Education and Rehabilitation, 1971.

Gula, Martin. Community service and residential institutions for children. *Children Today,* 1974, 21(6), 15–17.

Gunzberg, H. C. Institutionalized people in the community: A critical analysis of a rehab scene. *Research Exchange and Practice in Mental Retardation,* 1975, 1(1), 36–50.

Halpern, A., G. O'Connor, and D. Linsley. *The Identification of Problem Areas in the Establishment and Maintenance of Community Residential Facilities for the Developmentally Disabled.* Working Paper 64, Rehabilitation, Research and Training Center in Mental Retardation, University of Oregon, Eugene, 1973.

Hawkins, Donald E., and Geneva S. Folson. *Life Skills for the Developmentally Disabled: An Approach to Accountability in Deinstitutionalization.* Vol. I: *Project Summary and Evaluation Report.* Washington, D.C.: George Washington School of Medicine, 1975.

Helsel, Elsie D. Residential service. *Works on Mental Retardation.* New York: Grune & Stratton, 1971.

Helsel, Elsie D. Critical issues in the habilitation of mentally handicapped persons: 1975–1980. *Journal of Developmental Disabilities,* 1974, 1(2), 15–75.

Hopperton, Robert. *Technical Assistance Handbook for Community Officials.* Columbus, Ohio: Ohio State University College of Law, Law Reform Project in Developmental Disability Law, November 1975.

Hopperton, Robert. *Zoning for Community Homes: Handbook for Local Legislative Change.* Columbus, Ohio: Ohio State University College of Law, Law Reform Project in Developmental Disability Law, November 1975.

Kugel, R., and Wolf Wolfensberger (eds.). *Changing Patterns in*

Residential Services for the Mentally Retarded. Monograph of the President's Committee on Mental Retardation. Washington, D.C.: U.S. Government Printing Office, 1976.

Lewder, E., et al. *Five Models of Foster Family Group Homes: A Systematic View of Foster Care.* New York: Child Welfare League of America, 1974.

Manula, Richard A., and Nate Newman. *Community Placement of the Mentally Retarded.* Springfield, Ill.: Charles C Thomas, 1973.

National Association for Retarded Citizens. *The Right to Choose: Achieving Residential Alternatives in the Community.* Washington, D.C.: Residential Services and Facilitation Committee, NARC, 1973.

National Institute on Mental Retardation. *Guidelines for the Preparation of Proposals for the Establishment of Comprehensive Community Service (COMSERV) Experimental and Demonstration (E&D) Projects for Persons with Developmental Handicaps.* Toronto, Can.: Canadian Association for the Mentally Retarded, 1974.

Nelson, Ronald, et al. Community consideration in the evaluation of a children's residential treatment center. Paper presented at the American Psychological Association, Montreal, Canada, August 1973.

Nove, Kozen M. Toward independent living for the mentally retarded. *Social Work,* 1975, 20, 286–290.

O'Connor, Gail. *Home is a Good Place: A National Perspective of Community Residential Facilities for Developmentally Disabled Persons.* Washington, D.C.: American Association on Mental Deficiency, 1976.

O'Connor, Gail, and E. George Sitker. Study of a new frontier in community service: Residential facilities for the developmentally disabled. *Mental Retardation,* 13, 1975, 35–39.

Phelps, W. Vocational rehabilitation and deinstitutionalization of the mentally retarded. Paper presented at the West Virginia Division of Vocational Rehabilitation, Charleston, W. Va., 1974.

Philbrick, Dorothy. *Establishing Community-Based Homes for Developmentally Disabled Adults.* Redwood City, Cal.: Life Skills, Inc., 1974.

Public Affairs Committee, Inc. *Independent Living: New Goal for Disabled Persons.* Washington, D.C.: Public Affairs Committee, Inc., 1975.

Rhodes, Cindy. *A Sociological Challenge to Normalization as Applied To Community Alternative Residential Facilities.* Eugene, Ore.: Rehabilitation, Research and Training Center in Mental Retardation, University of Oregon, 1975.

Seevers, Charles J. An evaluation of the efforts of group home living. *Research Exchange and Practice in Mental Retardation,* 1975, 1(1), 51–65.

Sigelman, Carol (ed.). *Group Homes for the Mentally Retarded.* Lubbock, Texas: Texas Tech University Research and Training Center in Mental Retardation, 1973.

Soeffing, Marylane. Families for handicapped children: Foster and adoptive placement programs. *Exceptional Children,* 1975, 41(8), 537–543.

Stephens, Beth. Deinstitutionalization: A charge to special education. *Education and Training of the Mentally Retarded,* 1975, 10(3), 130–131.

Stickney, Patricia (ed.). *Gaining Community Acceptance: A Handbook for Community Residence Planners.* White Plains, N.Y.: Community Residence Information Senior Program (CRISP) of the Westchester Community Service Council, 1976.

Thompson, Marie McGuire. *Housing for the Handicapped.* Washington, D.C.: National Association of Housing and Redevelopment Officials, 1976.

Turner, Suzanne. *Guidelines for the Establishment of a Community Group Home.* Columbus, Ohio: Ohio Development Disabilities, Inc., 1974.

U.S. Comptroller General. *Report to the Congress: Returning the Mentally Disabled to the Community: Government Needs to Do More.* Washington, D.C.: U.S. Government Printing Office, 1977.

U.S. Superintendent of Documents (comp.). *People Live in Houses: Profiles of Community Residences for Retarded Children and Adults.* Washington, D.C.: U.S. Government Printing Office, 1975.

"How-To-Do-It" Issues

Evans, David, and Gerald Provencal. *Resident Manager Training: A Curriculum for Educating Foster Parents and Group Home Personnel.* Oakland, Cal.: Macomb-Oakland Regional Center, 1975.

Fisher, Gary. *Residential Training for Developmentally Disabled Adults: Individual Program and Assessment Guide for Residential Training Programs.* Columbus, Ind.: United Developmental Service, 1975.

Holland, Joanne F. (ed.). *Operating Manual for Residential Services Personnel.* Columbus, Ohio: Nisonger Center for Mental Retardation and Developmental Disabilities, 1974.

Kansas Department of Social and Rehabilitation Services. *Reintegration Handbook: A Continuum of Care,* 1974.

Macomb-Oakland Regional Center. *Family Care Training Homes: Manual of Procedures,* 1974.

Scheerenberger, R. *Managing Residential Facilities for the Developmentally Disabled.* Springfield, Ill.: Charles C Thomas, 1974.

Sigelman, Carol, and P. Werder. *Supervising Group Homes and Halfway Houses.* Lubbock, Tex.: Texas Tech University Research and Training Center in Mental Retardation, 1974.

C. ADVOCACY

Herr, Stanley S. Advocacy: The Missing Link to Fundamental Rights and Services. Washington, D.C.: Georgetown University Health Policy Center, 1977. (Mimeographed)

Mickenburg, Neil H. Starting a Legal Advocacy Project for Persons with Developmental Disabilities. Washington, D.C.: Georgetown University Health Policy Center, 1977. (Mimeographed)

Moore, Marie. *A Demonstration of Three Models of Advocacy of DD Children.* Milwaukee, Wisc.: United Cerebral Palsy Association, 1974.

National Association for Retarded Citizens. *Avenues to Change.* Vol. 1: *Effective Advocacy*; Vol. II: *Citizen Advocacy for Mentally Retarded Children: An Introduction.* Washington, D.C.: Bureau of Education for the Handicapped, DHEW, 1974.

National Institute of Mental Health. Conference proceeding, *Community Living Arrangements for the Mentally Ill and Disabled: Issues and Options for Public Policy.* Washington, D.C.: DHEW, 1976.

Neufeld, G. R., et al. Components of a Statewide Advocacy System. Washington, D.C.: Georgetown University Health Policy Center, 1977. (Mimeographed)

Ross, E. Clarke. Deinstitutionalization—National efforts in consumer advocacy and monitoring: The United Cerebral Palsy Association experience. Paper presented at the annual meeting of the American Association on Mental Deficiency, 1976.

Sigelman, Carol K. (ed.). *Protective Services and Citizen Advocacy.* Monograph 3. Lubbock, Tex.: Texas Tech University, Research and Training Center in Mental Retardation, 1974.

Sigelman, Carol K. A Machiavelli for planners: Community attitudes and the selection of a group home site. *Mental Retardation,* 1976, 14(1), 26–29.

Stearns, James C. Legislative Background of State Protection and Advocacy Systems for the Developmentally Disabled. Washington, D.C.: Georgetown University Health Policy Center, 1977. (Mimeographed)

D. COSTS OF AND FUNDING FOR RESIDENTIAL AND SUPPORT SERVICES

Bonn, Ethel M. The Impact of Redeployment of Funds of a Model State Hospital. *Hospital and Community Psychiatry,* 1975, 26(9), 584–586.

Cohen, Julius S. (ed.). *Benefit Cost Analyses for Mental Retardation Programs: Theoretical Consideration and a Model for Application.* Ann Arbor, Mich.: University of Michigan, 1971.

Conley, Ronald W. *The Economics of Mental Retardation.* Baltimore: Johns Hopkins University Press, 1973.

Copeland, William C., et al. *Funding Federal Money for Children: Title XX and Other Programs.* New York: Child Welfare League of America, 1975.

Desimone, Anthony S. Individualizing rehabilitation plans for cost-effective gains. *Social and Rehabilitation Record,* December 1974–January 1975, 2, 24–26.

Jones, Kenneth J., and Priscilla Pitt Jones. *The Measurement of Community Placement Success and Its Associated Costs.* Interim Report 2. Medford, Mass.: Florence Heller School for Advanced Studies in Social Welfare, Brandeis University, 1976.

Jones, Kenneth J., and Priscilla Pitt Jones. *A Cost Disaggregation for Children with Developmental Disabilities Attending Public Schools in Massachusetts.* Interim Report 3. Medford, Mass.: Florence Heller

School for Advanced Studies in Social Welfare, Brandeis University, 1976.

Litvia, Mark, and James Wilson. Medicaid: An Overview with Implications for the Developmentally Disabled. Working paper 95. Eugene, Ore.: Rehabilitation Research and Training Center in Mental Retardation, University of Oregon, 1976.

Paul, James L., Donald J. Stedman, and G. R. Neufeld (eds.). *Deinstitutionalization: Program and Policy Development.* New York: Syracuse University Press, 1977.

Piasecki, Joseph R., Jane E. Pittenger, and Irwin D. Rutman (eds.). *Determination of Costs of Community-Based Residential Programs.* Philadelphia: Horizon House Institute for Research and Development, 1976.

Silber, Stanley C. (ed.). *Multiple Source Funding and Management of Community Mental Health Facilities.* Selected papers from NIMH Regional Funding Conferences, 1970–1972. Washington, D.C.: U.S. Government Printing Office, 1972.

Sills, Malcolm. The transfer of state hospital resources to community programs. *Hospital and Community Psychiatry,* 1975, 26(9), 577–581.

Social Security Administration, Office of Research and Statistics. *Financing Mental Health Care Under Medicare and Medicaid.* Washington, D.C.: U.S. Government Printing Office, 1971.

U.S. Department of Health, Education, and Welfare, Office for Handicapped Individuals. *Federal Assistance for Programs Servicing the Handicapped.* Washington, D.C.: U.S. Government Printing Office, 1976.

E. LEGAL RIGHTS

Allen, Richard. *Legal Rights of the Disabled and Disadvantaged.* Washington, D.C.: National Citizens Conference on Rehabilitation of the Disabled and Disadvantaged, Social and Rehabilitation Service, 1969.

Bradley, Valerie J., and Gary J. Clarke (eds.). *Paper Victories and Hard Realities: The Implementation of the Legal and Constitutional Rights of the Mentally Disabled.* Washington, D.C.: Georgetown University Health Policy Center, 1976.

Krambs, Robert. *Litigation vs. Legislation in the Right to Treatment/Habilitation for Mentally Retarded Persons: A Review and Proposal.* Eugene, Ore.: Rehabilitation Research and Training Center in Mental Retardation, University of Oregon, 1976.

Mental Health Law Project. *Legal Rights of the Mentally Handicapped* (Vols. 1–3). Washington, D.C.: Mental Health Law Project, 1973.

President's Committee on Employment of Handicapped People. *A Handbook on Legal Rights of Handicapped People.* Washington, D.C.: U.S. Government Printing Office, 1976.

Turnbull, H. Rutherford, III, and Anne P. Turnbull. Deinstitutionalization and the law. *Mental Retardation,* 1975, 13(2), 14–20.

F. SPECIFIC STATE GOVERNMENT REPORTS*

General State Resources

National Association of Coordinators of State Programs for the Mentally Retarded, Inc. *Organization of State Services for the Mentally Retarded: A Source Book.* Arlington, Va.: NACSPMR, 1973.

President's Committee on Mental Retardation. *Mental Retardation: Trends in State Services.* Washington, D.C.: U.S. Government Printing Office, 1976.

Specific State Reports

California

Barnes, Delores, Pamela Krochalk, and John Hutchison (eds.). *Final Report: Comprehensive Community Residential Care System Study.* Los Angeles, Cal.: California State Department of Health and Exceptional Children's Foundation, 1976.

Barter, James T. Sacramento County's experience with community care. *Hospital and Community Psychiatry,* 1975, 26(9), 587–589.

California Instructional Television Consortium (Sonoma, California: California State University and Colleges). *Way to Go.* Baltimore: University Park Press, 1978.

California Legislature. Public Hearing on House Resolution 53, *A Review of California's Programs for the Developmentally Disabled.* November 1975.

California Legislature. State Hospitals Utilization Project Report, January 1976.

California Legislature. Quality Services Alternatives Report (Vols. 1 and 2). March 1976.

California Legislature. Assembly Bills 3800–3809 creating the Lanterman Developmental Disabilities Services Act. March 1976.

California Legislature Assembly Permanent Subcommittee on Mental Health and Developmental Disabilities. Rates of Payment for Services to the Developmentally Disabled. November 1975.

California Legislature Assembly Permanent Subcommittee on Mental Health and Developmental Disabilities. Planning and Community Service for the Developmentally Disabled. December 1975.

California Legislature Assembly Permant Subcommittee on Mental Health and Developmental Disabilities. Rates for Community Care Facilities for the Developmentally Disabled. March 1976.

Elpers, John R. Orange County's Alternative to State Hospital Treatment. *Hospital and Community Psychiatry,* 1975, 26(9), 589–592.

A Report to the State Assembly on Developmentally Disabled in California, 1972.

---

* Subcategories include (by state): community-based services, evaluation, legal problems, and state plans.

Colorado

Graves, James, and Angela Yawn. *Community Group Homes for the Mentally Retarded: Utilization of Evaluation Results for Program Planning and Quality Control.* Denver, Col.: Division of Mental Retardation, 1974.

Georgia

Georgia Association for Retarded Citizens. *A Study of Georgia Institutional Services for the Mentally Retarded and a Plan for Deinstitutionalization.* Atlanta, Ga.: Association for Retarded Citizens, 1975.

Georgia Department of Human Resources. *Behavioral Inventory and Training Plan for Day Training Centers for the Mentally Retarded.* Atlanta, Ga.: Division of Mental Health and Mental Retardation, 1976.

Graf, G. Thomas, and John O'Brien. A Model for Change: Atlanta, Georgia's Community Services Act. *Mental Retardation*, 1973, 13(5), 23–25.

Illinois

Arthur Bolton Associates. *A Report to the House Committee on the Developmentally Disabled.* Springfield, Ill.: Illinois House of Representatives, 1972.

Indiana

Division on Mental Retardation and Other Developmental Disabilities, Indiana Department of Mental Health. *Regulations for Alternate Residential Services.* Indianapolis, Ind.: Department of Mental Health, 1974.

Indiana Mental Retardation Residential Services Planning Project. *Our Human Resources* (Final Report). June 1972.

Maine

Bureau of Mental Retardation. *Planning Alternatives to Institutions: Report on a New England Case Conference.* Augusta, Me.: Bureau of Mental Retardation, 1974.

Burns, M. (ed.). *Pineland Center Program Guide (Vol. 1).* Pownal, Me.: Pineland Center, 1974.

Maryland

Residential Care Committee. *The Establishment of Community Based Residential Services for the Mentally Retarded of Montgomery County, Md.* Bethesda, Md.: Montgomery County Association for Retarded Children, 1971.

Reveley, Patricia M. *Deinstitutionalization: Problems and Opportunities.* Baltimore: Project SHARE, Department of State Planning, 1976.

U.S. General Accounting Office. *Deinstitutionalization of the Mentally Disabled in Maryland,* DHEW Region III (Draft Report), July 1976.

Massachusetts

Massachusetts Department of Mental Health. *Community Programs for Mentally Retarded People in Massachusetts.* Boston: Department of Mental Health, 1975.

Massachusetts Developmental Disabilities Council. *Fiscal Year 1977 State Plan for the Provision of Services and Facilities for Persons with Developmental Disabilities.* Boston: Developmental Disabilities Council, 1976.

Massachusetts Mental Hospital Planning Project. *Community Mental Health and the Mental Hospital.* Boston: United Community Planning Project, 1973.

Michigan

Final Report of the Joint Legislative Committee to Study Community Placement in Michigan, April 1976.

Harris, Gail A., and Sharon K. Miller. *A Plan for Improved Services for the Developmentally Disabled in Michigan.* Lansing, Mich.: Michigan Association for Retarded Citizens, 1974.

Michigan Senate. *Report of the Michigan 78th Legislature.* Senate Special Committee to Study the Problems and Needs of Adults with Developmental Disabilities, 1976.

Michigan State Office of Health and Medical Affairs. *Community Placement Program: An Examination of Programs and Outcomes of Community Placement of Adults and Children from Mental Health Institutions in Michigan.* Part 1—Report; Part 2—Technical Appendix. Lansing, Mich.: State Office of Health and Mental Affairs, 1974.

U.S. General Accounting Office. *Community Placement of the Mentally Disabled in Michigan,* DHEW Region V (Draft Report). July 1976.

Minnesota

Ad Hoc Committee on Community Alternatives. *Developing Community-Based Residential Alternatives: A Manual for Prospective Developers.* Minneapolis: Department of Public Welfare, MH/DD Program Office, 1976.

Minnesota State Planning Agency, Developmental Disabilities Program. *Community Alternatives and Institutional Reforms.* Minneapolis: State Planning Agency, 1975.

Reagan, M. *Establishing community alternatives in Minnesota.* Unpublished paper, 1974.

Salzberg, Charles L., and Don. R. Thomas. The Minnesota Learning Center Model: Institutional reform leading to deinstitutionalization and development of community alternatives. Paper presented at the Governor's Conference on the Handicapped, St. Paul, October 1974.

Missouri

Arthur Bolton Associates. *Developmentally Disabled in Missouri: Problems and Recommendations.* Sacramento, Cal.: Arthur Bolton Associates, 1975.

Nebraska

Arthur Bolton Associates. *Mental Retardation Services: An Analysis and Recommendations, Region V—Nebraska.* Sacramento, Cal.: Arthur Bolton Associates, 1973.

U.S. General Accounting Office. *Nebraska's Efforts to Provide Alternatives to Institutional Care for the Mentally Disabled,* DHEW Region VII (Draft Report). July 1976.

New Jersey

Arthur Bolton Associates. *An Analysis of Factors Which Predict Admission and Readmission to Institutions and Community Programs—Fiscal Analysis*; and *Analysis of Residents of State and County Hospitals in New Jersey.* Trenton, N.J.: Mental Health Planning Committee, 1975.

New Mexico

New Mexico Department of Hospitals and Institutions. *New Mexico Standards for Community Residential Facilities for the Developmentally Disabled.* Santa Fe, N.M.: Department of Hospitals and Institutions, 1974.

North Carolina

Division of Mental Health Services. *Adult Group Home Procedure Manual.* Raleigh, N.C.: Division of Mental Health Services, 1974.

Ohio

Butler, Hattie, and Suzanne Turner (eds.). *Community Living for Ohio's Developmentally Disabled Citizens.* Columbus, Ohio: Ohio Developmental Disabilities, Inc., March 1974.

McAvoy, Nancy Clark, and Suzanne Turner. *Community Living for Ohio's Developmentally Disabled Citizens.* Vol. 2: Technical Assistance Manual. Columbus, Ohio: Ohio Developmental Disabilities, Inc., May 1975.

Ohio Developmental Disabilities Inc. *Residential Options for Ohions with a Developmental Disability.* Proceedings of Residential Seminar II, Columbus, Ohio, 1975.

Shapiro, Helen. Circle of homes: Group homes for the retarded in Cuyahoga County. *Mental Retardation,* 1975, 13(3), 19–21.

Oregon

Burling, Edward, et al. *Deinstitutionalization in Oregon: A Review of Services Within the Human Resources System.* Portland, Ore.: Project SHARE, Department of Human Resources, 1975.

Morton, William O., and Robert Muse. *Deinstitutionalization Initial Report.* Portland, Ore.: Project SHARE, Department of Human Resources, 1975.

U.S. General Accounting Office. *Deinstitutionalization of the Mentally Disabled in Oregon,* DHEW Region X (Draft Report). July 1976.

Pennsylvania

Arthur Bolton Associates. *An Analysis of Pennsylvania's Program for the Mentally Retarded.* Harrisburg, Pa.: Department of Public Welfare, 1973.

Ashbaugh, John W., et al. *Northeast Pilot Area Patient, Staff and Cost Projections.* Washington, D.C.: Warburton, Ashbaugh and Associates, 1975.

Baldwin, Norman. *Project MAIN: An Intensified Training for Staff in Community Residences.* Harrisburg, Pa.: Office of Mental Retardation, Department of Public Welfare, 1976.

Byrne, Jane M. (ed.). *Early Intervention Program Resource Guide: Selected Readings from Programs for Young Disabled Children in Pennsylvania.* Harrisburg, Pa.: Office of Mental Retardation, Department of Public Welfare, 1976.

Department of Public Welfare. *Office of Mental Retardation Draft Concept of State Plan.* Harrisburg, Pa.: Department of Public Welfare, 1976.

Pennsylvania Association for Retarded Citizens. *As Close As Possible—A Study of Community Residences for Retarded Adults.* Harrisburg, Pa.: Association for Retarded Citizens, 1973.

Pennsylvania Association for Retarded Citizens. *Report of the PARC Ad Hoc Committee for Resolution II: A Design for Living.* Harrisburg, Pa.: Association for Retarded Citizens, 1974.

Pennsylvania Association for Retarded Citizens. *Action Plan for Community Services.* Harrisburg, Pa.: Association for Retarded Citizens, 1976.

Pennsylvania Comprehensive Mental Health Planning Committee. *Toward Complete Integration.* Harrisburg, Pa.: Mental Health Planning Committee, 1976.

Pennsylvania Office of Mental Retardation. Community Living Arrangements for Citizens Who Are Mentally Retarded: Implementation Packet. Harrisburg, Pa.: Department of Public Welfare, 1977. (Mimeographed)

Pennsylvania Office of Mental Retardation. Proposed Interpretation of Administrative Policies and Practices for ICF/MR Facilities Serving Fifteen Persons or Less (CLA's). Harrisburg, Pa.: Department of Public Welfare, 1977. (Mimeographed).

Rhode Island

Maluccio, Anthony U. *Community-Based Residential Programs—A Study of Alternatives to Deinstitutionalization.* Providence, R.I. Interdepartmental Task Force on Community-Based Programs, 1975.

Rhode Island Department of Mental Health, Retardation and Hospitals. *Project Alternatives—Retardation (P.A.R.).* Providence, R.I.: Department of Mental Health, Retardation and Hospitals, 1976.

South Carolina

South Carolina Department of Mental Retardation. *Region IV Staff Development Conference on Institutional Reform.* Columbia, S.C.: Department of Mental Retardation, 1973.

Virginia

Arthur Bolton Associates. *Virginia's Mental Health and Mental Retardation System: The Next Steps.* Sacramento, Cal.: Arthur Bolton Associates, 1975.

Northern Virginia Association for Retarded Citizens. *Community Residential Options: Developing and Operating Group Homes for the*

Developmentally Disabled of Virginia. Arlington, Va.: Association for Retarded Citizens, 1975.

Virginia Department of Mental Health and Mental Retardation. *Developmentally Disabled Plan for Virginia—FY 1975.* Richmond, Va.: Department of Mental Health and Mental Retardation, 1974.

Virginia Department of Mental Health and Mental Retardation. *Guidelines to Community Residential Programming for the Mentally Handicapped.* Richmond, Va.: Department of Mental Health and Mental Retardation, 1974.

Virginia Housing Development Authority. *Housing Assistance Payments Program Description for Housing for the Adult Mentally Retarded, New Construction and Substantially Rehabilitated Housing, Existing Housing, Section 8.* Richmond, Va.: Housing Development Authority, 1976.

Washington

Department of Social and Health Services. *Capital Construction Master Plan.* Olympia, Wash.: Bureau of Developmental Disabilities, 1976.

Wisconsin

Wisconsin Department of Health and Social Services. *Guidelines to Community Living Systems for the Developmentally Disabled.* Madison, Wisc.: Department of Health and Social Services, 1975.

G. BIBLIOGRAPHIES ON MENTAL RETARDATION, DEINSTITUTIONALIZATION, AND COMMUNITY CARE

Dickson, Claudia. *Legal Rights of the Mentally Retarded Citizen* (Bibliography series 1). Arlington, Tex.: National Association for Retarded Citizens Library, 1974.

Dickson, Claudia. *Community Based Residential Services* (Series 11). Washington, D.C.: National Association for Retarded Citizens, 1975.

Larsen, Lawrence. *Community Residences for the Mentally Retarded: Bibliography and Abstracts.* Chapel Hill, N.C.: DD Technical Assistance System.

Marker, Gail R. *Hospitalization v. Non-Hospitalization: A Review of the Social Service and Psychiatric Literature.* Washington, D.C.: Mental Health Law Project, 1974.

Program for the Analysis of Deinstitutionalization Resources. *Reintegrating Mentally Retarded People into the Community: An Annotated Bibliography of Print and Audiovisual Information and Training Materials.* Reston, Va.: Council for Exceptional Children, 1975.

APPENDIX II
Major Federal Court Rulings

A. PROMINENT CASES

Bell v. Wayne County General Hospital, 384 F.Supp. 1085 (E.D. Mich. 1974).
Boddie v. Connecticut, 401 U.S. 371 (1971).
Brown v. Board of Education, 347 U.S. 483 (1954).
Davis v. Watkins, 384 F.Supp. 1196 (N.D.Ohio 1974).
Dixon v. Attorney General, 325 F.Supp. 966 (M.D.Pa. 1971).
Eisenstadt v. Baird, 405 U.S. 438 (1972).
Griswold v. Connecticut, 381 U.S. 479 (1960).
Gross v. State of Hawaii, Civ. Action No. 43090 (Cir.C.Ha.) Consent decree 2/3/76.
Harper v. Virginia Board of Elections, 383 U.S. 663 (1966).
Heryford v. Parker, 396 F.2d 393 (10th Cir. 1968).
Horachek v. Exon, 357 F.Supp. 71 (D.Neb. 1973).
In re Ballay, 482 F.2d 648 (D.C. Cir. 1973).
In re Gault, 387 U.S. 1 (1967).
Jackson v. Indiana, 406 U.S. 715 (1974).
Lake v. Cameron, 364 F.2d 657 (D.C. Cir. 1966).
Lessard v. Schmidt, 349 F.Supp. 1078 (E.D.Wisc. 1972), vacated, 414 U.S. 473 (1974), on remand 379 F.Supp. 1376 (E.D.Wisc. 1974), vacated on other grounds, 421 U.S. 957, 95 S. Ct. 1943 (1975).
Lynch v. Baxley, 386 F.Supp. 378 (M.D.Ala. 1974).
Nathan v. Levitt, No. 74 CH 4080 (Cir. Ct., Cook Co., Ill.) Consent order 3/26/76.
New York State Association for Retarded Children and Parisi v. Rockefeller, 357 F.Supp. (E.D.N.Y. 1973), order entered as *NYSARC and Parisi v. Carey,* 393 F.Supp. 715 (E.D.N.Y. 1975).
O'Connor v. Donaldson, 422 U.S. 563 (1976).
Palko v. Connecticut, 302 U.S. 319 (1937).
Patients v. Camden County Board of Freeholders, N.L. 33417-74 PW (N.J. Super. Ct.) 5/19 and 10/12/76.
Ricci v. Greenblatt, Civil No. 72-469-F (D.Mass., 1972).
Rouse v. Cameron, 373 F.2d 451 (D.C. Cir. 1966).
Stanley v. Illinois, 405 U.S. 645 (1972).
Welsch v. Likens, 373 F.Supp. 487 (D.Minn. 1974).
Wyatt v. Stickney, 344 F.Supp. 373 and 387 (M.D.Ala. 1972 aff'd sub. nom.), *Wyatt v. Aderholt,* 503 F.2d 1305 (5th Cir. 1974).

B. SELECTED CASES BY SUBJECT*

Civil Commitment

Legal principle	Leading federal case
Right to effective assistance of adversary counsel—appointed if necessary—at all significant stages	*Lynch v. Baxley; Heryford v. Parker*

* Full citations are given for those cases not listed in the preceding section.

Legal principle	Leading federal case
Prior notice	Due process requirement—14th Amendment; *Lessard v. Schmidt*; *Dixon v. Attorney General*
Prompt preliminary hearing	*Lynch v. Baxley*; *Lessard v. Schmidt*; *Bell v. Wayne County General Hospital*
Right to prompt full judicial hearing	*Lessard v. Schmidt*; *Bell v. Wayne County General Hospital*; *Lynch v. Baxley*
Right to be present at hearings, confront and cross-examine adverse witnesses	6th Amendment rights in criminal rights
Right to testify and compel the testimony of witnesses	General subpoena powers, 14th Amendment
Right to remain silent	5th Amendment right in criminal rights; *Lessard v. Schmidt*; *Lynch v. Baxley*
Standards of proof	Stricter than "preponderance of the evidence" in ordinary civil cases, either "clear and convincing evidence," or "beyond a reasonable doubt"; *In re Ballay*; *Lessard v. Schmidt*
Right to trial by jury	*Lynch v. Baxley*
Right to a full record	14th Amendment
Grounds for commitment, either: 1. Dangerous to self or others, or 2. Incapable of surviving safely in the community with family or friends	*O'Connor v. Donaldson* (Note: some district courts also require proof of a recent "overt act" where dangerousness is involved); *Lessard v. Schmidt*; *Bell v. Wayne County General Hospital*; *Dixon v. Weinberger*
Use of least restrictive alternative	*Shelton v. Tucker* (generally); *Lessard v. Schmidt*; *Lynch v. Baxley*; *Welsch v. Likens*; *Wyatt v. Stickney*; *Dixon v. Weinberger*
Regular review of necessity for institutionalization	*O'Connor v. Donaldson*

Personal Constitutional Rights

Constitutional right	Leading case
Right to privacy—including right to marry; but also including	*Griswold v. Connecticut* (over 40 states have laws restricting the

more broadly the right to be free from wrongful intrusion that would cause harm to a person of ordinary sensibility	mentally retarded from marrying)
Right to beget children (a part of the right to privacy)	*Eisenstadt v. Connecticut* (over 25 states have laws permitting sterilization of the mentally retarded, and some sterilizations are performed every year)
Right to raise children (extends to unmarried fathers)	*Stanley v. Illinois* (over 40 states do not require consent of the retarded parents before adoption of their children—few even require prior notice)
Right to vote	*Harper v. Virginia Board of Election* (most states restrict incompetents from voting, holding office or serving on a jury, though the law is rarely enforced)
Right to contract	A common law right which would be applicable to the states through the 14th Amendment. However, common law usually restricted the right on an all or nothing basis, requiring the guardian to act in place of the incompetent person.
Free exercise of religion	1st Amendment
Freedom of speech	1st Amendment
Protection from unreasonable search and seizure	4th Amendment
Freedom of association	1st Amendment
Right to sue	*Boddie v. Connecticut* (most states usually require a guardian to appear in place of the "incompetent")
Right to refuse treatment	*Price v. Sheppard,* 239 N.W. 2d 905 (Minn. 1976)

Standards for Adequate Care

The standards imposed in these decisions are usually formulated through a process that involves the court, the plaintiffs, the defendents, and experts in the field of retardation. Quite often the standards imposed by the courts conform in many respects to model standards developed by professional organizations, e.g., the Joint Commission on Accreditation of Hospitals' *Standards for Residential Facilities for the Mentally Retarded* (1971; revised, 1977), and the American Association on Mental Deficiency's *Standards for State Institutions for the Mentally Retarded* (1964—now under revision).

The following section sets out selected examples from the standards that have been imposed in four major cases involving institutions for the retarded: *Wyatt v. Stickney, New York State Association for Retarded Children and Parisi v. Rockefeller, Welsch v. Likens,* and *Davis v. Watkins* (which simply adopted *Wyatt* standards). Some of the standards imposed are quantifiable, e.g., staffing requirements, while others address resident's rights, treatment philosophies, and standards of care. Standards imposed by the courts deal not only with the institution itself but also with issues such as who may be admitted to the institution and placement of residents in the community. The standards set forth in these decisions are very extensive in scope and are quite detailed. They reach into every facet of institutional life and beyond, including intake, physical plant, nutrition, staff number, distribution, shift schedules, training, resident care and treatment, record-keeping, etc. The actual court orders themselves are far more lengthy and detailed than even these examples would seem to imply.

Staff

Standard		Case
"As soon as such persons become available and in no event later than . . . [date] there shall be employed at . . . the Hospital professional staff reflecting the following staff-resident ratios:		*Welsch v. Likens*
"Registered nurses		
"Severely or profoundly retarded	1:40	
"All other residents	1:100	
"Physicians (licensed to practice in the state)	1:75	
"Physical therapists (licensed to practice in the state)	1:100	
"Speech and hearing therapists (with at least a bachelor's degree)	1:100	
"Social workers (with at least a bachelor's degree)	1:50	
"Psychologists (with at least a master's degree)	1:100	
"Dentists (licensed to practice in the state)	1:350"	
". . . the following direct care staff-resident shift ratios shall be attained by . . . not less than 1:4 during waking hours and 1:8 at night in medical units and in those units serv-		*Welsch v. Likens*

ing nonambulatory residents, and not less than 1:4 during waking hours and 1:6 at night in those units serving ambulatory residents who are under the age of 18, severely or profoundly retarded, or emotionally disturbed . . ."	
"All employees with direct care responsibilities shall be able to communicate in English. Sufficient bilingual staff shall be hired to serve the needs of Spanish-speaking residents."	*New York State Association for Retarded Children and Parisi v. Rockefeller*
"Willowbrook shall employ and maintain sufficient therapy aides at the grade 7 and 9 levels to ensure that the following numbers shall be present and on duty: "(a) During the hours of the day and evening when residents are awake: "(1) One therapy aide for every four residents in buildings primarily for residents who are children, nonambulatory or multiply handicapped, and for those residents receiving intensive psychiatric care; "(2) One therapy aide for every sixteen adult residents presently residing in buildings 19 and 32; "(3) One therapy aide for every resident receiving an intensive behavior modification program; "(4) One therapy aide for every six residents of buildings not covered above."	*New York State Association for Retarded Children and Parisi v. Rockefeller*

Resident Care and Treatment

Standard	Case
"Residents have a right to habilitation including medical treatment, education and care, suited to their needs, regardless of age, degree of retardation or handicapping condition."	*Wyatt v. Stickney*
"Each resident at . . . Hospital shall be provided with an individualized habilitation, or program, plan and programs of training and remedial services as specified in Department of Public Welfare Rule 34 . . . and these plans	*Welsch v. Likens*

Standard	Case
shall be periodically reviewed, evaluated, and where necessary, altered to conform to the condition of the particular resident."	
"As part of his habilitation plan, each resident shall have an individualized post-institutionalization plan."	*Wyatt v. Stickney*
". . . shall maintain a contract for acute medical care with one or more accredited hospitals. In addition, service agreements with backup medical facilities shall be developed, where appropriate."	*New York State Association for Retarded Children and Parisi v. Rockefeller*
"Mistreatment, neglect or abuse in any form of any resident shall be prohibited. The routine use of all forms of restraint shall be eliminated. Physical restraints shall be employed only when absolutely necessary to prevent a resident from seriously injuring himself or others."	*New York State Association for Retarded Children and Parisi v. Rockefeller*
"Parents, relatives or guardians shall be notified in writing whenever restraints are used."	*New York State Association for Retarded Children and Parisi v. Rockefeller*
"Individualized physical therapy services on a regular basis . . . shall be provided to those residents who can benefit therefrom . . ."	*New York State Association for Retarded Children and Parisi v. Rockefeller*
"Speech pathology and audiology services shall be provided as needed, to all residents."	*New York State Association for Retarded Children and Parisi v. Rockefeller*
"Each resident shall have at least annually a comprehensive medical examination."	*New York State Association for Retarded Children and Parisi v. Rockefeller*
"Each resident at Willowbrook shall receive appreciable and appropriate attention each day from the direct care staff in his living unit, whose primary responsibility shall be the care and development of each resident."	*New York State Association for Retarded Children and Parisi v. Rockefeller*

Physical Facilities

Standard	Case
"All ambulatory residents shall sleep in single rooms or in multi-resident rooms of no more than six persons. The number of nonambulatory residents in a multi-resident room shall not exceed ten persons. There shall be allocated a minimum of 80 square feet of floor space per resident in a multi-resident room. Screens or curtains shall be provided to ensure privacy. Single rooms shall have a minimum of 100 square feet of floor space."	*Wyatt v. Stickney*
"Living areas shall be sectioned and partitioned so that no more than eight residents live or sleep in one unit."	*New York State Association for Retarded Children and Parisi v. Rockefeller*
"Residents shall be encouraged to decorate their living areas and furniture."	*New York State Association for Retarded Children and Parisi v. Rockefeller*
"There shall be one toilet and one lavatory for each six residents . . . Soap and towels and/or drying mechanisms shall be available in each lavatory. Toilet paper shall be available in each toilet facility."	*Wyatt v. Stickney*
"There shall be one tub or shower for each eight residents. If a central bathing area is provided, each tub or shower shall be divided by curtains to ensure privacy."	*Wyatt v. Stickney*
"Defendants shall provide living facilities which afford residents privacy, dignity, comfort and sanitation."	*New York State Association for Retarded Children and Parisi v. Rockefeller*
"Air conditioning shall be installed . . . Carpeting shall be installed in the day-rooms, dormitories, stairwells, corridors and activity rooms in all residential living areas . . ."	*Welsch v. Likens*

Physical Plant and Maintenance

Standard	Case
"The institution shall meet such provisions of the Life Safety Code of the National Fire Protection Association as are applicable to it."	*Wyatt v. Stickney* and *New York State Association for Retarded Children and Parisi v. Rockefeller*
"Defendants shall establish and maintain a program of adequate maintenance of buildings and equipment which shall include prompt elimination of existing maintenance backlogs."	*New York State Association for Retarded Children and Parisi v. Rockefeller*
"Regular housekeeping and maintenance procedures which will ensure that the institution is maintained in a safe, clean, and attractive condition shall be developed and implemented."	*Wyatt v. Stickney*
"The temperature in the institution shall not exceed 83° F nor fall below 68° F."	*Wyatt v. Stickney*

Records

Standard	Case
"There shall be a system of records for each resident, developed and maintained under the supervision of a competent librarian or registrar."	*New York State Association for Retarded Children and Parisi v. Rockefeller*
"These records shall include: "(a) Identification data including the resident's legal status . . . "(c) An inventory of the resident's life skills . . . "(k) A monthly summary of the extent and nature of any work activities and the effect of such activity upon the resident's progress . . . "(l) All team minutes relating to the resident . . ."	*Wyatt v. Stickney and New York State Association for Retarded Children and Parisi v. Rockefeller*

Food and Nutritional Services

Standard	Case
"The diet for residents shall provide at a minimum the Recommended Daily Dietary	*Wyatt v. Stickney*

Allowance as developed by the National Academy of Sciences."	
"Consistent with their capabilities and handicaps, residents shall be taught to feed themselves and shall be fed both hot and cold foods and beverages in a normal fashion with due regard for personal hygiene . . ."	*New York State Association for Retarded Children and Parisi v. Rockefeller*
"Residents shall be provided with the least restrictive and most normal living conditions possible. This standard shall apply to dress, grooming, movement, use of free time, and contact and communication with the outside community . . ."	*New York State Association for Retarded Children and Parisi v. Rockefeller*
"Each resident shall have his own clothing, which is properly and inconspicuously marked with his name, and he shall be kept dressed in this clothing."	*Wyatt v. Stickney*
"Residents shall be entitled to send and receive sealed mail."	*Wyatt v. Stickney*
"Teeth shall be brushed daily with an effective dentifrice. Individual brushes shall be properly marked, used and stored."	*Wyatt v. Stickney*
"Unless there is a medical order to the contrary, a minimum of two hours per day of recreation activities shall be provided for each resident, and weather permitting, recreation activities shall take place outdoors."	*New York State Association for Retarded Children and Parisi v. Rockefeller*
"No resident shall be required to perform labor which involves operation and maintenance of the institution . . ."	*Wyatt v. Stickney*

Education of Residents

Standard	Case
"Residents have a right to receive suitable educational services regardless of chronological age, degree of retardation or accompanying disabilities or handicaps."	*Wyatt v. Stickney*
"School-age residents shall be provided a full and suitable educational program. Such	*Wyatt v. Stickney*

Standard	Case
educational program shall meet the following minimum standards:	

	Mild	Moderate	Severe/ profound
Class size	12	9	6
Length of school year (in months)	9–10	9–10	11–12
Minimum length of school day (in hours)	6	6	6

Standard	Case
"Each resident in a formal education program shall have an individual education plan which shall specify short term and long term objectives. The education staff shall consult on at least a weekly basis with those individuals and teams responsible for the daily care and programming of each resident."	*New York State Association for Retarded Children and Parisi v. Rockefeller*
"Toilet training shall not be a prerequisite to receiving educational services."	*New York State Association for Retarded Children and Parisi v. Rockefeller*

Medication

Standard	Case
"No medication shall be administered unless at the written order of a physician."	*Wyatt v. Stickney*
"Residents shall have a right to be free from unnecessary or excessive medication."	*New York State Association for Retarded Children and Parisi v. Rockefeller*
"Medication shall not be used as punishment, for the convenience of staff, as a substitute for program or in quantities that interfere with the resident's program."	*Wyatt v. Stickney* and *New York State Association for Retarded Children and Parisi v. Rockefeller*

Admission Standards

Standard	Case
"No mentally retarded person shall be admitted to the . . . Hospital following a judicial	*Welsch v. Likens*

order for civil commitment if services and programs in the community can afford adequate habilitation to such person."

"No borderline or mildly retarded person shall be a resident of the institution." *Wyatt v. Stickney*

APPENDIX III
Values, Ends, and Criteria

Policy/value	End	Criteria
Equal justice	Full legal and civil rights for the developmentally disabled	Are developmentally disabled persons represented by counsel in proceedings for involuntary commitment? Guardianship? Conservatorship? Abuse or mistreatment?
		Are developmentally disabled persons informed of their rights in treatment facilities in ways which they can understand?
		To the extent of their capabilities, are developmentally disabled persons given the right to make decisions affecting their lives? Vote? Marry? Manage their own funds?
		Do conservatorship and guardianship procedures adequately protect the rights of those developmentally disabled persons judged incompetent to manage their own affairs?
	Equal access to publicly supported generic services	Are developmentally disabled persons granted access to public education programs on a nondiscriminatory basis?
		Are developmentally disabled persons granted equal access to generic human service resources such as social services, recreation, health maintenance, income maintenance, public residential programs, etc.?
	Elimination of discrimination against otherwise qualified developmentally disabled persons in gainful employment	Do mechanisms exist for the recruitment and placement of developmentally disabled persons in gainful employment?
		Are employers held legally responsible for discriminating against the developmentally disabled?
		Does a developmentally disabled person have access to the judicial process if he or she has been discriminated against?

Policy/value	End	Criteria
Human dignity	Participation in the development of service plans by developmentally disabled clients	Are developmentally disabled persons informed of the treatment and habilitation options available to them? Are their views regarding the nature of services to be provided solicited?
	Provision of care and habilitation services which afford privacy and which maximize the self-respect of the client	Do developmentally disabled residents of residential facilities have access to private storage space for personal possessions? Are residents allowed to wear their own clothes? Are residents encouraged to carry out those self-help and self-care tasks which they are capable of performing? Do sleeping arrangements afford any privacy to the resident?
	Opportunity to communicate with others to the full extent of each developmentally disabled person's ability	Are residents given access to phones? Are they allowed to send and receive mail? Do training programs maximize communication skills?
Equity	Equal distribution of support and other services regardless of where client resides	Do developmentally disabled persons in institutions have access to the same level of educational, social, and health services as similar persons residing in the community? Is the converse also the case? Do developmentally disabled persons in rural communities have access to the same level of service as those in urban areas? Low income vs. high income areas?

	Allocation of resources to developmentally disabled persons based on need rather than level of disability	Are persons with more severe disabilities receiving services to meet their needs? Are persons with severe disabilities accepted into programs serving the less severely disabled (e.g., vocational rehabilitation)?
Individualization	Establishment of diagnostic and evaluation services geared to an individual assessment of client needs, strengths, and disabilities	Do multidisciplinary diagnostic and evaluation programs exist in each area of the state? Are clients and families aware of the existence of such facilities? Can persons at all levels of income afford such services? Are diagnostic services linked to direct service agencies in the community?
	Preparation of an individualized treatment and habilitation plan for all developmentally disabled persons	Is an individualized treatment and habilitation plan developed for each client when he or she enters the system? Do individualized plans include the full array of services needed to maximize the client's potential? Is the responsible agency capable of securing or purchasing those services in the plan that are not available from that agency? Does the client and his or her family participate in the development of the plan? Are individualized plans monitored to determine their continuing relevance? Are plans modified to reflect changing needs?
	Development of services which maximize individual functioning	Can the service system accommodate the movement of staff and/or clients from less to more independent settings?

Policy/value	End	Criteria
		Is the system capable of evaluating progress on some level of functioning continuum?
		Can the system provide the necessary training and support to assist in self-help skills development? Resocialization? Self-care skills?
Normalization	Integration of developmentally disabled persons into more normal community living whenever possible	Are developmentally disabled persons, alone or in groups, allowed access to more normal living arrangements in the community?
		Are developmentally disabled persons living in the community encouraged to participate in regular community activities such as recreation?
		Are services for the developmentally disabled located in more integrated areas of the community or are they grouped with other services for disadvantaged persons?
		Do transitional programs exist for developmentally disabled persons which aid clients in "coping" with community living?
		Do programs exist that aid in changing community attitudes regarding the needs of developmentally disabled persons?
		Are adequate support services available to developmentally disabled persons to ensure that they can be maintained in the community?

	Development of physical facilities that are smaller and more normal in appearance	Do new service facilities for developmentally disabled persons at the state and local levels reflect a change in orientation from larger to smaller facilities? Are state standards sufficiently flexible to make smaller facilities economically feasible? Have larger, more institutional facilities been modified to include smaller, more manageable units? Do reimbursement schemes encourage the development of such facilities?
	Development of programs that are age and disability appropriate	Are services organized so that like age groups are served together? Are services and activities appropriate to age and level of disability?
Least restrictive setting	Placement of developmentally disabled persons in settings that are appropriate to their needs and that allow them the maximum amount of freedom	Are persons residing in unnecessarily restrictive settings being prepared to move to less restrictive settings? Does a sufficient spectrum of facilities exist to accommodate the needs of persons at varying levels of disability? Does some mechanism exist that allows for an assessment of an individual's residence and service needs prior to placement?
	Development of residential facilities that minimize the utilization of physical restraints	Do procedures exist that spell out the limited uses and conditions for physical restraint or isolation? Are all avenues of intervention exhausted before the application of restraints on freedom? Is the use of drugs as a method of restraint controlled? Are such drugs used only when appropriate?

Policy/value	End	Criteria
Right to treatment	Provision of residential treatment and habilitation services that meet generally recognized standards	Does each client in a residential facility have an individualized treatment plan? Are sufficient trained and qualified staff available to carry out the service plan? Is the plan monitored regularly to determine progress? Is the status of the resident monitored regularly to determine whether placement in an alternative facility or program is required? Does the resident have access to ancillary services such as recreation, physical therapy, occupational therapy, and vocational training? Do grievance procedures exist that make it possible for the resident or his or her representative to draw attention to inadequacies or abuses?
Protection from harm	Elimination of harmful, exploitative, or potentially life- or health-threatening conditions	Are the health needs of developmentally disabled persons receiving services attended to on a regular basis? Are developmentally disabled persons protected from potentially harmful experimentation? Are sanitary and health standards enforced in all care facilities? Are support services for developmentally disabled persons residing in the community sufficient to prevent the exploitation and/or abuse of such clients? Are residential facilities in the community located in areas that minimize potential exploitation and/or abuse of developmentally disabled residents?

Efficiency/economy	Minimize the time entailed in bringing resources to bear on the needs of developmentally disabled persons	Are generic and other community-based services accessible to the developmentally disabled in a reasonable period of time? Are there waiting lists? Are residential services available to developmentally disabled persons within a reasonable period of time? Generic services to persons in residential care? Waiting lists? Are services available to developmentally disabled persons at the earliest possible time to ameliorate and perhaps prevent subsequent long-term disability?
	Minimize the amount of money spent to administer and deliver the services needed by the developmentally disabled	Are the costs of various units of service as economical as possible? Are total administrative and service costs as economical as possible? Are third-party payors, taxpayers, county, state, and federal government shares of the total cost proportional to their capacity for support?
	Maximize the utilization of existing personnel and capital resources on behalf of the developmentally disabled	Is the proportion of direct service to administrative staff as high as it might be? Are there overlapping and duplicative services being offered to the developmentally disabled consumer? Is the developmentally disabled client receiving the maximum feasible amount of professional direct service time? Does the allocation of existing resources correspond to the priorities of need among the developmentally disabled population (functionally and geographically)? Do those concerned with the administration and provision of services to the developmentally disabled have convenient access to administrators and providers?

Policy/value	End	Criteria
Effectiveness	Develop and deliver those services to the developmentally disabled that are expected to have the greatest relative impact in terms of the aforestated goals	Is the state sponsoring those services expected to have the greatest relative impact on the developmentally disabled? Are prevention, detection, and early intervention services available to developmentally disabled persons at the earliest possible time in order to ameliorate and perhaps prevent subsequent long-term disability? Does the mix of services provided match the service needs (potentials) of the developmentally disabled? Are the services as accessible as they could be to the developmentally disabled population? Are the relative impacts of services on the developmentally disabled being evaluated? Are the results being considered in developmental disabilities program planning and funding decisions?

INDEX

Accountability, fluctuating, 10
Admission, involuntary, in context of deinstitutionalization, 20–21
Advocacy, 113–114
Agencies involved in deinstitutionalization, 28–32
Alternatives, less costly, for deinstitutionalization, 98–100

Background of deinstitutionalization, 1–12

Canadian National Institute on Mental Retardation, 71
Caregivers, 9–10
Choices, critical, in planning for deinstitutionalization, 51–57
Civil rights, 21–22
Client management system, coordinated, 104–114
Commitment procedures, 21
Consent in context of deinstitutionalization, 22–23
Context of deinstitutionalization, 14–47

Deinstitutionalization
- background of, 1–12
- context of, 14–47
- evidence of inadequate planning for, 9–11
- history of, 1–12
- ideology vs. implementation, 7–9
- implementation of, 7–9, 84–115
- planning for, 48–82
- summary, 116–120

Developmental Disabilities Act, 36
Developmental Disabilities Authority, 28–30
Diagnosis in implementation of deinstitutionalization, 107–108
Dignity, human, in context of deinstitutionalization, 17
Disabled, developmentally, deinstitutionalization of: *see* Deinstitutionalization

Economy in context of deinstitutionalization, 18
Education
- family, 99–100
- right to, 24–25

Effectiveness in context of deinstitutionalization, 18
Efficiency in context of deinstitutionalization, 18
Endorsements in planning for deinstitutionalization, 72–75
Enforcement of quality standards, 104
Equity in context of deinstitutionalization, 17
Evaluation
- in implementation of deinstitutionalization, 107–108
- in planning for deinstitutionalization, 78–81

Family aide, 99
Financing, "hand-me-down," 9
Follow-up, 112–113
Funding
- federal, in context of deinstitutionalization, 32–36
- state, increasing the level of, 97–98
- use of all available, for deinstitutionalization, 92–94

Goal development in planning for deinstitutionalization, 57–61

History of deinstitutionalization, 1-12

Ideology of deinstitutionalization, 7-9
Implementation of deinstitutionalization, 7-9, 84-115
Individualization in context of deinstitutionalization, 17
Insecurity, parental, 9

Judicial imperatives in context of deinstitutionalization, 19-27
Justice, equal, in context of deinstitutionalization, 17

Licensing, 101-102

Management, implementation, 88-91
Medicaid, 34-35
Monitoring
as part of management process, 112-113
in planning for deinstitutionalization, 76-78

Needs, assessment of, in planning for deinstitutionalization, 61-66
Negotiation, in planning for deinstitutionalization, 72-75
Normalization in context of deinstitutionalization, 17

Organizational structure in context of deinstitutionalization, 27-32

Planning
for deinstitutionalization, 48-82
inadequate, for deinstitutionalization, 9-11
individual service, 108-109
predischarge, 110-112
Programs, federal, for deinstitutionalization, 38-47
Purchase of service, 72

Quality assurance in implementation of deinstitutionalization, 100-104

Rate setting in implementation of deinstitutionalization, 103-104
Rehabilitation, vocational, 35
Resources
development of, in implementation of deinstitutionalization, 91-100
identification and development of, in planning for deinstitutionalization, 66-72
redeployment of institutional, 94-97
Respite care, 99
Rights, personal, in context of deinstitutionalization, 21-22

Service procurement, 109-110
Services
access to generic, in context of deinstitutionalization, 24-25
adequacy of, in context of deinstitutionalization, 23-24
generic, expanding use of, 98
homemaker, 99
Socioeconomic factors in planning for deinstitutionalization, 67
Standard setting, 102-103
Strains and political conflicts during implementation process, 86
Supplemental Security Income, 34

Training, family, 99-100
Transitional phase in implementation of deinstitutionalization, 85

Transportation for
developmentally disabled, 99
Treatment, right to, in context of
deinstitutionalization, 18

Values, exploration of, in context of
deinstitutionalization, 15–19
Vocational rehabilitation, 35

Zoning and code restraints, 68